Imagining the End

Imagining the Evil

Imagining the End

Mourning and Ethical Life

Jonathan Lear

The Belknap Press of Harvard University Press

Cambridge, Massachusetts, and London, England

First Harvard University Press paperback edition, 2024
Second printing

Library of Congress Cataloging-in-Publication Data

Names: Lear, Jonathan, author.
Title: Imagining the end : mourning and ethical life / Jonathan Lear.
Description: Cambridge, Massachusetts : The Belknap Press of Harvard University
Press, 2022. | Includes bibliographical references and index.
Identifiers: LCCN 2022005773 | ISBN 9780674272590 (hardcover) |
ISBN 9780674297333 (pbk.)
Subjects: LCSH: Bereavement—Moral and ethical aspects. |
Grief—Moral and ethical aspects. | End of the world—Moral and ethical aspects. |
Life—Moral and ethical aspects. | Gratitude.
Classification: LCC BF789.D4 L375 2022 | DDC 155.9/37—dc23/eng/20220412
LC record available at https://lccn.loc.gov/2022005773

For Gabriel and Sophia and Sam with love

Contents

Preface

In writing this book, I have regularly been visited by the phrase *even here*. Socrates meets someone in the midst of daily life, but he does not just move on. His life exudes confidence that if he lets the conversation develop, *even here* philosophy will arise. And though psychoanalysis differs in important ways from Socratic conversation, it too holds to the commitment that if one will allow a report of some ordinary event to unfold, *even here* something of human significance will show up. A number of chapters in this book contain ordinary, fleeting moments.

This book circulates around a cluster of questions that I have found, somewhat to my surprise, hang together. How does the *end of life* in the sense of world catastrophe fit with the *end of life* in the sense of life's purpose, aim, or meaning? What is the difference between healthy and unhealthy uses of our imagination? How do we live with the realization that cultures—traditionally providers of solace and meaning—are themselves vulnerable? What is mourning—and how could it be part of our flourishing? How is it that remarkable individuals grab our imaginations—and then stay with us throughout our lives? What is gratitude, and what is its place in human life? In thinking about these questions, I found myself wondering again about the psychoanalytic concept of repetition. So that is another question: What is repetition?

One of the pleasures of writing a book is that one gets to share one's thoughts with people one has not met and cannot otherwise reach. Another is to continue a conversation with a friend but at some geographical or temporal distance. It is a special mixture of intimacy and separation. To those who read this book and find they get something out of it, I would like to express my gratitude.

"So Socrates!" he teased, "you are still saying the
same things I heard you say long ago."
Socrates replied: "It is more terrifying than that:
Not only am I always saying the same things,
but also *about* the same things."

(Xenophon, *Memorabilia* IV.4.6)

Imagining the End

Imagining the End

1

We Will Not Be Missed!

The Moment

Not long ago, I listened to a lecture on climate change. The lecture went as one might expect. There was a warning of impending ecological catastrophe and talk of the "Anthropocene," suggesting that our age—the age in which humans dominate the Earth—is coming to an end. At the end of the talk, there was a discussion period. At one point, a young academic stood up and said simply, "Let me tell you something: We will *not* be missed!" She then sat down. There was laughter throughout the audience. It was over in a moment.

The comment was experienced as a joke, and the laughter was spontaneous. It was a moment of release that no one anticipated but which the audience shared. Release from what? If we read newspapers or participate in social media, read blogs, or watch television, it would be surprising if the end of the world were not somehow on our minds. Indeed, there is cultural pressure to feel anxious about the future. Does this anxiety help us, perhaps by alerting us to the challenges we face? Or might it distract us or otherwise get in the way?

Two Senses of an End

The joke links together two different senses of what we might mean by *the end of life*. There is the obvious sense of the end as *termination,* of life coming to an end. But there is also the sense of end as the *aim* or *purpose,* the *goal* or *telos* of life; the sense of what life is all about. In effect, the joke "says" that it is because we have lost a sense of our proper end—our purpose—that human life is coming to an end.

The official meaning of the statement is one of cosmic justice (rendered in comic form). We will not be missed because we do not *deserve* to be missed. We humans, during our tenure on Earth, have been so greedy and avaricious, so thoughtless, aggressive, and destructive that if the endangered species and rain forests and polluted rivers, the plastic-choked lakes and oceans could speak, they would say, "*good riddance!*" The rest of the world is better off without us. It was as though the human presence on Earth had been a disruption, and natural harmony would be restored once we were gone.

The joke also picks up on a culturally shared anxiety about the end of democracy. Are the contemporary institutions of democratic political life able to withstand the polarizing pressures that have come to mark our time? Again, there is a fear of democracy coming to an end because of the loss of our shared sense of its *purpose* or *end.* And, if we take Plato as a guide, these two catastrophes—one ecological, one political—are likely linked to each other by the phenomenon of human appetite. For Plato, our appetites are voracious and unlimited; they can undergo indefinitely many transformations in imagination. They seek to acquire and consume without any sense of proper end. Democracy, for Plato, is precisely the political form that inflames our appetites and encourages us to expand them without limit. Were Plato to observe our scene today, it would make sense to him that democracy comes to an end, ushering in a tyranny of appetites that itself brings ecological catastrophe.

The Joke

Still, one might well wonder how we are able to enjoy this imagined punishment as a joke. On the surface, the comment invites us to envisage the catastrophic destruction of human life on Earth: how does that get to be funny? The humor is dark, and it depends on the double meaning in the phrase "We will not be missed!": we will not be missed because we do not deserve to be missed, and we will not be missed because none of the creatures who survive will be capable of missing us in the manner that being missed matters to us. Other animals suffer loss and grieve, sometimes in complex and heartrending ways. Our pets may miss us. But in the joke, we are threatened with the loss of the special kind of missing that is characteristic of human beings: mourning. We shall investigate mourning throughout this book, but to begin, when a loved one dies, our imaginations get busy, trying to make sense of it all. Often, we join in cultural rituals; sometimes, we withdraw. Either way, our imagination and emotional life seeks the whole: Who was that person? What was our relationship? What does it all mean?

We symbolize and daydream, make judgments and play around; sometimes, we cry our hearts out. Mourning is a living-on in the hearts and minds of others in the characteristic ways we humans miss others.[1] It is, of course, not unusual for humans when facing the prospect of our own deaths to find solace in the thought that we will be remembered lovingly by our loved ones, and fondly and admiringly by those with whom we have shared our life. It is important to us to think of ourselves as participating in values and projects that we take to be good and believe will continue after we are gone. So, it seems that the punishment we suffer in the imaginary logic of the joke is that of being deprived of this kind of being missed. If humans go out of existence, we will not be missed because *the very capacity to miss* in this way will go out of existence at the same time. There will be nobody left to miss us. How could that thought be funny?

Where Are We?

If not being missed is an imagined punishment for our misdeeds, it helps to ask from what position might we enjoy the prospect of this punishment. There are occasions in which we say "We are . . . ," and although we thereby officially include ourselves, through an indeterminateness of mind, we at the same time unofficially leave ourselves out. Consider the self-righteous preacher standing before his congregation who declaims, "We are all sinners!" If he is put on the spot by a member of the congregation—"Really? *Even you, Reverend?*"—he will say, "Yes, of course! *Me most of all!*" But what if he is not put on the spot? It is not difficult to envisage a situation in which the preacher *leaves it in abeyance* whether he is *really* included in this "we." In a similar vein, both Kierkegaard and Heidegger have shown us that we typically use phrases such as

"We are all going to die someday" or "We are all mortal" as clichés to *tranquillize us out* of any real encounter with how what we are saying targets us. Although we say "we," a stealthy "I" slips the noose.

The joke plays with this ambiguity in where we might locate ourselves. There is of course the *we* who will not be missed, the *we* who are the official subject of the judgment, the *we* who are about to get what we deserve. But what about *we who render the judgment?* Well, if pushed by this question, we have to admit we fall into both categories. But the joke works by allowing us a moment to leave that question in abeyance. There is room in imagination—*in fantasy*—for us to take up the position of *we* as *judge* and leave it unemphasized that we are also the judged. Sigmund Freud called it a split in the ego—in which one part sets itself over against another and judges it. In this case, a bare judging consciousness speaks on behalf of the world, declaring it will be better off without us. In imagination, we project ourselves forward to a time in which "we" can imagine us getting what "we" deserve, only somehow, in *the exercise of the joke itself,* we are on the *punishing* rather than on the receiving end of the punishment. There is pleasure to be had in imagining justice done, due punishment meted out to humankind—at no real cost to one's split-off self. Note that, spoken from the world-superego position, "We will not be missed!" has legislative force, tinged with omnipotence. It is like the king saying of his prisoner, "He will spend the rest of his days in prison." So, it is not simply a statement about the future; it is an enactment of an (imaginary) punishment in the present.

It also makes room for an imaginary escape hatch in which although *we* deserve the punishment, somehow, I get to be the one doing the punishing (and enjoying it).

On the Receiving End

Thus far, I have been exploring the pleasures to be had in enjoying "We will not be missed!" as a joke. Now I would like to consider the joke from the other side of the split and inquire into the punishment we are to suffer. In one sense, the answer is obvious: sometime in the not-too-distant future, we will suffer the fate of not being missed. But as a psychoanalyst, I am trained to ask: What is going on *now*—in the moment of telling the joke—that might serve as a punishment?

There are two uncanny features of the joke that are not yet accounted for. First, the manner of not being missed is unusual. By way of contrast, consider a familiar trope to be found in films of the "Wild West": a bad guy comes to town and threatens the emerging but fragile system of justice. After some worries and real peril to the town, he is killed by a good guy. As a few of the citizens stand over the grave a character actor says, "He will not be missed." The point is that civilization has been saved, and the bad guy will not be part of it. But in the situation we are considering, it is not just that civilization is under threat, civilization is also the bad guy—responsible for its own undoing.

Second, in the standard case, the bad guy is not missed but the social institution of mourning continues—and that is part of why not being missed matters. Being remembered, mourned, honored is a persisting good. But in the case of the death of all humanity, we are confronted with the prospect of the end of mourning itself. We, the hearers of the joke, are thus to be the last generation of mourners. Insofar as there is any mourning left to be done, we have the last chance. Does that come with any responsibilities? Ought we to be mourners of ourselves? If we *will* not be missed, should we start missing ourselves *now*, in anticipation?

We would then become subject and object of our own mourning activity.

Here, we come to a distinctive moment in the joke—one that marks it off from merely being dark humor and which lies at the other end of the emotional spectrum from providing us with the comic relief of an imaginary escape hatch from our problems. In effect, this strand in the joke "says" that it is *too late*. Not just that it is too late to reverse the tide of events, but that it is too late to do anything now that would make it worth our being mourned. And so, the imaginary punishment in the joke is not simply being deprived of the good of being missed by others in the future, nor is it even the punishment of having to imagine now that we will be deprived of the good of being missed. In addition, the joke enjoins us to acknowledge that even our current activity of mourning—should we exercise our capacity to mourn ourselves— would, in these circumstances, be of no value. It is an attack on the value of our current capacities. At stake is not just not being missed *in the future* but the value of missing *in the present*.

The Mis-Anthropocene

This strand of the joke is an expression of despair. Examining it is important because we live in an age that fosters it. In the name of drawing attention to the problems we face, there is a form of discourse that discourages creativity and hope in addressing them. Despair thrives when it is not fully conscious of what it is. It portrays itself as truthfulness—as the courage to face grim reality straight on, without the wishful illusions that keep us so complacent. It does not understand its own motivated fantasy structure.

In the joke, the "we who will not be missed" deserve what is coming our way. This *we*, as I have suggested, must be a split-off *we*—separated in fantasy from all that is marvelous and good about us: our capacity for generosity and kindness, for stunning acts of creativity, for achievements of discovery and knowledge, for art and love, for our capacity to understand and appreciate self-consciously the world in which we live. If all this human goodness were present to mind, the young academic's comment would be an occasion for overwhelming sadness, especially if combined with the poignant recognition that in some sense we have brought this destruction on ourselves. In short, it would be an occasion for mourning—for facing up to our ambivalence about our own situation and at least beginning to work through a sense of tragic loss. This is the mourning that is foreclosed in the joke. And so, there is reason to see the joke as an active *refusal to mourn*.

It is this refusal that marks the joke off from other attempts at humor or witty aphorisms about the limits of mourning. For example, in an episode from The Simpsons, an ageing Grandma chooses heroic death, killing a dragon. Young Lisa says:

"If Grandma lives on in our hearts, she will never be truly gone."

And her skeptical brother Bart responds:

"Until we die, then it will be like she never existed."[2]

In this scene, Bart confronts us with a blunt truth about the human condition, but there is no hint that she or they are worthless or that they are getting what they deserve. In the episode, Grandma is a hero. The comedy plays with our wishful illusions about immortality—it brings out the distance between illusion and reality in comic fashion—but it works without derision or contempt or punishment. On the contrary, it is an example of our marvelous human ability to take tough truths and turn them into humor.

And here is a comment from Bernard Williams and Friedrich Nietzsche: "Nietzsche . . . got it right when he said that once upon a time there was a star in a corner of the universe, and a planet circling that star, and on it some clever creatures who invented knowledge; and then they died and the star went out, and it was as though nothing had happened."[3] There is, again, no implication that we are being punished or getting what we deserve. The "once upon a time . . ." is a familiar genre that allows the author freedom from taking any particular point of view. This is an allegory in which the creatures have not done anything bad—if anything, they have done something remarkable by inventing knowledge. And then, the lights go out—*not* in response to anything those creatures have done, good or bad. The lights just go out. This image may be tough to take, but it is told in a manner that philosophers used to call a "spiritual exercise"; something we could grow from by learning to face it. There is no pressure internal to the aphorism to move in the direction of despair.

By contrast, in "We will not be missed!" we are being punished, we deserve to be punished, and nothing we could do about it now—*including mourning*—could possibly alter our miserable fate. So, this leads us to the question: What is it about mourning that tempts us to refuse it?

There are, I think, three overlapping sets of answers. First, there is pleasure to be had in imagining ourselves on the right side of justice, inflicting punishment on those who we think deserve it. This pleasure fuels a tendency toward misanthropy—enjoyment of a generalized dislike of human beings and the human condition. And it is easier to enjoy misanthropy if one has a split-off conception of the human—as greedy, selfish, thoughtless animals. I also wonder whether the joke deals with our shared anxiety about the future by gratifying a wish *to get it all over with.*[4] At least we would then no longer have to bear the anxiety of not knowing. In this context, I want to mention the concept of the "Anthropocene." In itself, the concept is legitimate and important: it helps us to conceptualize an age in which humans have had an overwhelming influence on the world. But it is possible for a legitimate concept to be put to misanthropic use: notably, to express a desire to get the whole thing over with.

Second, there may be too much pain involved in acknowledging the loss caused by our own extinction. We need to stay away from it—and if that means diminishing our own worth by portraying us one-sidedly in diminished terms, that may be easier to bear. There is also an element here that is difficult to admit because it goes against current cultural images—a sadness that if we were all to perish, all the goodness we create and contribute every day would disappear from the universe. And all memory of our goodness would vanish without a trace.

And this brings us to the third reason: the refusal to mourn sustains despair. Despair nourishes itself via its refusal to mourn. In this strand of the joke, "We will not be missed!" is part of a self-maintaining activity of despair—a resoluteness in hopelessness. To see how this is so, we need to understand in more detail what mourning is and how, by its own activity, mourning takes the energy out of despair.

Mourning as Health

The first step is to recognize mourning as a manifestation of human health. Sigmund Freud placed the capacity to mourn at the center of human well-being. In "Mourning and Melancholia," he identi-

fied mourning as the healthy counterpart to the pathological condition of melancholia. But his focus was on pathology: he wanted
to come to understand the strange phenomenon of melancholia
by comparing it to what he took to be a familiar aspect of life, "the
normal affect of mourning."[5] So, there is still a question of what
it is about our *normal* life that makes mourning healthy. Freud
says that mourning typically involves "grave departures from the
normal attitude to life," and yet "it never occurs to us to regard
it as a pathological condition." But the reason he gives is forward looking: "We rely on its being overcome after a certain
lapse of time."[6] On this view, mourning would be healthy only
in the extended sense of being efficacious in *getting us back* to
ordinary forms of life.

But there is also a strain in Freud's thought that is intrigued by
the inner workings of mourning itself. In brief, he argues that we
humans have a "capacity for love"—he gives it a scientific name of
libido—which, in the course of our development, we exercise by
forming loving attachments to people and things in the world. Our
loved ones are of course vulnerable, and should a loved one die,
we *suffer* loss: we linger over memories, we experience grief, we turn
to rituals to help us understand and contain our sorrow, and we
let our minds wander. "But *why it is that this detachment of libido
from its objects should be such a painful process is a mystery to us* and
we have not hitherto been able to frame any hypothesis to account
for it. We only see that libido clings to its objects and will not renounce those that are lost even when a substitute lies ready to hand.
Such then is mourning."[7] Freud here takes the stance of a natu-
ralist, purportedly observing us without presupposition as he would
observe any other species. What sticks out for him as needing explanation is why, when we suffer loss, do we spend time mourning,
rather than just find another and move on?

The Freudian answer, implicit in his work, is that it is characteristic of us as erotic creatures to come to life when a loved one dies. We get busy emotionally, imaginatively, and cognitively and at least try to make sense of what has happened by creating a meaningful account of who the other person was, what the relationship has meant, and how it continues to matter. We mourners, through our suffering, transform what would otherwise be a mere change into a loss, by which I mean the special emotion-filled way we create and maintain an absence in the world. We maintain this absence by keeping emotions, memories, and imagination active, by keeping the loss present to mind.

Why should this activity constitute our flourishing? At the opening of the *Metaphysics,* Aristotle famously says that all humans by nature desire to understand. Mourning shows that even at the extreme of suffering the death of a loved one, we are active trying to understand the meanings of our attachments. This activity counts as healthy because seeking to understand via making meaning is our characteristic activity; it is how we flourish, even in times of pain and grief.

But the psychoanalytic understanding of mourning takes us far beyond the paradigm moment at the grave. Once we understand the erotic dynamics of attachment and separation and loss, we are in a position to see that mourning *broadly understood* is pervasive in human life. Indeed, it is constitutive of human development.[8] Allow me to tell you about the day my teddy bear ate a Ritz cracker. I had left teddy with a cracker by his side, and when I came back, it was gone. I wish I had the words that would convey my amazement and delight. Maybe *he really did eat the cracker*! Of course, at some point, I "outgrew" teddy—I "left him behind" as we say—but delightful memories of this moment have been coming back to me, from time to time, throughout my life. These are playful moments, and reverie is built into them. But here is the thing: although I can delight in remembering how it seemed to me then, *that* remembering cannot take me back to the experience of its actually seeming that way. Internal to the memory is not just delight but also poignancy: an awareness that this is a me that I can remember and imagine but never really get back to. That manner of experiencing the world—a manner of living that once constituted a boy who was me—is gone. The point is not just that human development consists in different stages of cognitive and emotional experience, but also that such development itself consists in bidding *adieu* to earlier forms of experiencing.

By now, it should be clear that from a psychoanalytic point of view, mourning and play are deeply intertwined. At first, it looks as though two scenes could not be more different than a child playing with a teddy bear and an adult mourning at a grave. But if we probe beneath the surface, we can see that even in play, the child is getting ready to say goodbye to his teddy; and it is not unusual for mourners to engage in reveries of continued conversations with the deceased loved one. It is Donald Winnicott who grasped what these phenomena have in common. He spoke of the need for "an intermediate area of experiencing . . . *that is not challenged,* because no claim is made on its behalf except that it shall exist as a resting place for the individual engaged in *the perpetual human task* of keeping inner and outer reality separate yet interrelated."[9] (He called this area "transitional," which I do not think is the best term, but it has stuck.) In the case of childhood play—say, with a teddy bear—Winnicott says that it is a matter of tacit agreement between good-enough parents and the supporting adult world that "*we will never ask the question: 'Did you conceive of this or was it presented to you from without?' The important point is that no decision on this point is expected. The question is not to be formulated.*"[10]

He notes it "will *always* be important" for us that we have "a neutral area of experience that will not be challenged."

That "neutral area" sometimes includes the graveyard. We friends and supporters of the mourners do not inquire into the status of ongoing conversation with the dead loved one, for example. The question is not to be raised. Winnicott says as much himself: "It is assumed here that the task of reality-acceptance is *never complete,* that no human being is free from the strain of relating inner and outer reality, and that relief from this strain is provided by an intermediate area of experience . . . which is not challenged (arts, religion, etc.) This intermediate area is in direct continuity with the play area of the small child who is 'lost' in play."[11] I take mourning to be included in his "etc."

Mourning and Morality

I am here talking about Morality with a capital M. "Morality," Bernard Williams tells us in *Ethics and the Limits of Philosophy,* "is not one determinate set of ethical thoughts. It embraces a range of ethical outlooks," but they all circulate around a "special notion of obligation."[12] Morality is in the business of producing punishment: "Blame is the characteristic of the morality system. The remorse or self-reproach or guilt . . . is the characteristic first-personal reaction within the system."[13]

It is striking how well this account fits with Freud's dark account of the civilizing process in *Civilization and Its Discontents.* Freud argues that civilization is not in place to promote our happiness or well-being, but rather to sustain itself, often at our expense. Basically, civilization makes strategic use of our capacity to form a superego. Our individual capacities for hatred and aggression and discontent are directed through cultural channels onto ourselves—

thus producing crippling guilt and inhibition—or are then directed outward onto fantasied images of the bad other, who is punitively punished and blamed.

Notice how easily the comment "We will not be missed!" fits into the morality system. We *will* not be missed because we do not *deserve* to be missed; and we do not deserve to be missed because we *could have done otherwise,* and we *should have done otherwise,* and we were thus *obligated to do otherwise.* Thus, we are to blame. We *ought* to feel guilt. But—and here comes the kicker—*it is too late to do anything about this now,* other, that is, than recognize the inevitable, recognize our guilt and suffer.

Mourning provides relief from all of this. Of course, many forms of behavior and emotional reaction are called mourning—including blaming the dead, feeling guilty or angry toward them, thinking they should have done otherwise, and so on. I do not wish to rule any of them out as cases of mourning. But I do want to draw attention to the special manner of mourning I have been describing: a play-like activity of imagination and memory in which the loved one is remembered. There may well be a partition into lovable and unlovable qualities. However, issues of blame and questions of what the dead person could or should have done otherwise are left in abeyance. This "transitional" form of mourning provides a respite from all that. And yet, it is just this manner of experience that the joke forecloses with respect to our mourning ourselves.

Mourning and the *Kalon*

Aristotle famously thought that happiness was the highest human good. And he thought that involved developing a character and being fortunate enough in circumstance that one could live an active life that was both excellent or virtuous and thereby, as he put it, *kalon*. The term *kalon* is translated sometimes as *noble*, sometimes as *beautiful*, sometimes as *fine*.[14] It is something that *strikes us* and fills us with admiration when we witness it, and it fills us with pride, a sense of accomplishment, and meaningfulness when we participate in it. This capacity to act in ways that are *kalon*, Aristotle thinks, distinguishes our human manner of flourishing—happiness—from the manners of flourishing of other animals.[15] We should not get hung up on the trope of how we differ from other animals—a topic surrounded by ignorance and caricature. The important point Aristotle is making is that there is something special about our capacity to act and create in ways that are *kalon*. The *kalon* is a crucial node of human experience: connecting the social experience of being recognized with respect and admiration with the personal satisfaction of knowing one is acting well—and everyone *getting it right* about the activity being *kalon*. In the *kalon*, self and society and world come together in a manifest harmony.

My aim here is not to re-create the life world in which the concept of the *kalon* had its home, nor to recover in detail what Aristotle meant. But it seems to me that he was getting at something important. I am going to use the term *kalon* as a signifier for a concept we may not yet have in fully accessible form. I shall explore the idea of an enigmatic good throughout this book. For now, let me give a modern example of *kalon* activity: a generous person living generously. There is a special sort of flourishing manifest here. First, generosity is a stable and integrated condition of a person's psyche. Generous people will be motivated to perform generous acts when appropriate occasions arise, and the generous acts will flow from and express their character. Second, generous people need to have good judgment as to how to express their generosity. Not just any act of giving will do. Third, living generously is truly a manner of our flourishing and is experienced as such—both by generous people themselves and by those around them. The generous life is itself satisfying, experienced as meaningful and worthwhile and, as such, pleasurable.

The Aristotelian-spirited thought is that this generous life is *kalon.* To put the point ironically but earnestly, there is something *marvelously* generous about generosity. It is not merely about the obvious benefit to the recipient or the satisfying experience of those who bestow generosity. It is not just that generosity is its own reward. And it is not just that generosity is constitutive of the generous person's flourishing (though it is). It is that this flourishing—this generous person's living generously—shines forth. It is not only good but wondrous that the universe contains generosity within it.

I would like to close by suggesting that mourning is itself *kalon.* It is not only good but wondrous that there should be mourning. As we have seen, mourning is a distinctively human way of responding to loss. It is a special manner of expressing grief—an insistence that what happened was not a mere change. The loss is testament to our previous attachments—love and hate, care and entanglements—and constitutes us as beings with a history, a history that continues to matter. In response to loss, we make meaning: re-creating in memory and imagination what we have lost and reanimating forms of life that might otherwise disappear. This seems to me a wondrous response to love and loss; a wonderous response to caring and finitude in general.

Part of what it is to mourn the *kalon*—in the sense of mournfully anticipating the *kalon* going out of existence—is to acknowledge that the universe will be impoverished in the sense that something good will have gone out of existence. I imagine the objections: "You are projecting value onto the universe!" and "It is

only from the human point of view that the *kalon* has any value."
These are importantly different objections, and I shall consider
them in order. The claim to be *projecting* value is in itself vague. It
has been given a precise meaning in a psychological-clinical context, but it functions as a metaphor outside that context. Insofar
as we can understand it, the claim in this case is false. We are not
anthropomorphizing the universe, nor are we treating it as though
it were a human subject. Rather, we are treating ourselves as den-
izens of the universe, however large and however incomprehensible it may yet remain to us. In mourning the *kalon,* we are recognizing it as good—and our mourning itself stands witness to the
fact that should mourning go out of existence, it would not be a
mere change in the universe; it would be a loss. It would be the
loss of loss.

This brings me to the second claim: that it is only from the
human point of view that the *kalon* has value. As far as we know,
that is true. But if it is only from the human point of view that
the *kalon* can be appreciated for what it is, that seems all the more
responsibility for us humans to express, celebrate, honor, remember,
and, if need be, mourn the *kalon* in anticipation. The fact that
judgment of the value of the *kalon* needs to come from the human
point of view does not of itself mean it is "merely subjective" in
any pejorative sense of that term.[16]

It seems to me that part of what it is to mourn the *kalon* in anticipation is to stand witness to its importance—that it should be,
period. Even if we do not yet know in detail what we can or should
mean by *kalon,* we can see that the joke works by attacking it. For
"We will not be missed!" to gain humorous assent in the sense that
we do not *deserve* to be missed, all that makes us *kalon*—our generosity, and kindness, and courage, and creativity—needs to be

passed over. It cannot be funny that the *kalon* recognized as such should go out of existence.

It is, of course, open to the young academic to respond that this whole idea of the *kalon* is a fiction, an idealization that ought to be rejected. From this point of view, truthfulness demands taking a dim view of the human condition, and the best one can do is turn this truth into humor. I cannot prove that this outlook is wrong. But I have tried to provide an interpretation of how this outlook gains its grip on us, one that I hope will loosen its charm, *and* to appeal to our own shared experience of the importance and value, the goodness of mourning. I am sympathetic to a remark made by the philosopher Bernard Williams and then reiterated by Cora Diamond: at some point, you have to decide *whose side you are on.* I have tried to come out on the human side. I hope at the least that I have shown that I *can* take a joke—I can take it so seriously and interpret it at such length as to drain the humor right out of it.

2

Transience and Hope
A Return to Freud in a
Time of Pandemic

The Long Trip

One day, when I was six years old, I got in the back seat with my sister, and our parents drove us to visit our grandparents. When we arrived, there was a party going on. Lots of grown-ups dressed up. My Grandma Jenny came over, bent down, and told me that her father, my great-grandfather, had gone off on a long trip. I barely knew who he was, and I had no idea why she was telling me this. A moment later, an older cousin walked over and said, "He's dead." This is the moment I realized adults lie to children.

Why do they do this? Well, "they" don't all. There have been cultural shifts, and my sense is that these days, adults try to be more honest with children. Still, this moment is worthy of attention. My grandmother was not a reflective person, and I suspect she acted from an ingrained habit that expressed a cultural norm. Officially, the norm was to protect children—in this case, from a knowledge

that would be too much for them at their age. But what knowledge is that? If my grandmother had said, "He died," I doubt I
would have learned much. What I did learn a moment later when
my cousin spilled the beans was that the topic of death was treated
by adults as dangerous, taboo, forbidden to children.

I am not here interested in my grandmother's psychology but
rather in a shared cultural imaginary of which she availed herself.
In acting as though there is some "adult knowledge" from which
one needs to protect the children, one tacitly reassures oneself
that one has something—namely, the knowledge that is not to be
passed on. But what knowledge is that? The cultural norm of protecting the children serves to protect *the adults* from recognizing
that in this painful and important moment in life, they understand little or nothing.

Being an adult, so understood, thus involves *playing* the role of
adult. It also allows gratifications of childhood play. When my
grandmother said her father had gone on a long trip, I now wonder
whether she was expressing *her* fantasy—that in playing the adult,
she was, at the same time, able to return to something from childhood. Perhaps her parents had told *her* that a grandparent had
gone on a long trip. The fantasy may have been passed through
the generations—the very words passing from adult to child—
without anyone particularly noticing. Perhaps my grandmother
was inviting me to join her in play—a transitional space of cultural experience in which we tacitly understand that the question
of whether he is *really* on a long trip is not to be asked. Ironically,
it was a child—my older cousin—who destroyed the play space
with the intrusion of reality: "He's dead."[1]

This vignette came back to mind in the first wave of the coronavirus pandemic. There is something amusing in the reversal of
roles. In this scene, it is the children who are able to face reality

and talk about it frankly; it is the adults who live in childlike fantasy. But there is more. We also recognize that Grandma Jenny is getting something right in turning to imagination and fantasy in response to the death of a loved one. And her imagination tends in the direction of reassuring herself (and perhaps others) about the stability of the world in the face of death. Her father might be gone, but *we are still here.* And the idea of *a long trip* presupposes stability in time and space: for something to be *a trip* one must be able to get from *here* to *there.* So, *here* needs to remain stable enough for us to imagine it as a place of departure; and the idea of a long trip is meant to be a comforting image of immortality: somehow life goes on in happy-enough circumstances, however vaguely understood. In short, we get to comfort ourselves about both *here* and *there.*

It is this background stability that came into question in the first wave of the pandemic. We cannot imagine a loved one on a long trip if temporality itself comes into question. But the coronavirus infected our sense of the future. In normal times, a sense of the future is implicit in everyday life. In a time of pandemic, by contrast, the future becomes uncanny. It is like peering into a fog: if we turn on the high beams, it only gets worse. Of course, life is always uncertain, and the future always holds surprises, but uncertainty is now much more closely present to mind.

Imagine a future generation looking back on us and telling our story. Here's the rub: we *cannot really do it*—at least, in any way that does not immediately seem to be one person's fantasy. We can imagine the narrative beginning, "They lived in a time of pandemic"; but then what? The pandemic has destroyed any shared illusion about how the future will unfold continuously from the present. And insofar as the meaning of our present is shaped by its future significance, the sense of the meaningfulness of the present must come into question. This, I believe, is a source of the anxiety so many feel.

In these extraordinary times, our ordinary practices become a matter of anxiety for the culture as a whole.

So, if I had been six years old in the pandemic's first wave, I would not have been able to get in the car with my parents and drive to my grandparents; I would not have been able to enter a crowded room of adults talking with each other up close. How would Grandma Jenny tell me her imaginary story? On Zoom? Would my cousin break the news using the private chat function? The first wave has waned, but the pandemic continues to unsettle us. We are anxious and uncertain about the future, and the past no longer provides clear guidance. The vulnerability of our normal practices has come into view.

Shattered Pride

I want to return to a three-page essay Sigmund Freud published just more than a century ago, in 1916, "On Transience." I have long thought it a classic. The essay presents itself as philosophical in the broad sense of that term, about a phenomenon *transience* that marks the human condition. When it comes to human beings, transience is not itself transient. It is not that I think this self-presentation false, but I do read the essay differently now, re-fracted through the pandemic. The essay now seems to me a pro-found *struggle* with the intrapsychic consequences of living through world catastrophe. Of course, catastrophes differ—and the geopolitical upheavals of World War I will not be the same as the world-historical consequences of the coronavirus pandemic, which we are only beginning to comprehend. Even so, it is now much clearer that this essay is *timely*, and in an uncanny fashion it is about *our time* in a way I could not have understood until I found myself living in our time.

Although one must read the essay from beginning to end, it is illuminating to try to understand it from back to front. Narratively, the story moves in linear fashion from earlier to later. It begins with a nostalgic reminiscence from the recent past: "Not long ago I went on a summer walk through a smiling countryside in the company of a taciturn friend and of a young but already famous poet."[2] The poet and Freud have a disagreement about the meaning of transience, and that takes up most of the essay. It concludes a year later, in the author's present as well as the present of the intended reader: in the midst of the World War I Europe. But try to think of that world catastrophe not as the denouement of this essay but as the problem that haunts it from the beginning. Freud is grappling with how to live with the radical uncertainty of the immediate future. In particular, can the structure of values that has shaped his world survive, even unto tomorrow?

Here is how Freud describes the world situation in which he is writing. It is the penultimate paragraph of his essay:

My conversation with the poet took place in the summer before the war. A year later the war broke out and robbed the world of its beauties. It destroyed not only the beauty of the countrysides through which it passed and the works of art which it met with on its path but it also *shattered our pride* in the achievements of our civilization, *our admiration* for many philosophers and artists and *our hopes* of a final triumph over the differences between nations and races. *It tarnished* the lofty impartiality of our science, it revealed our instincts in all their nakedness and let loose the evil spirits within us which we thought had been tamed forever by centuries of continuous education by the noblest minds. It made our country small again and made the rest of the world far remote. It *robbed us of very much that we had loved,* and showed us how ephemeral were many things that we had regarded as changeless.[3]

When I read this passage before the pandemic, it looked as though Freud was ruefully bringing to our attention that under the destructive pressures of war, even the achievements of art, science, and civilization show themselves to be fragile and transient (see Chapter 6). But now, as I reread it in the midst of this pandemic, I see that Freud is also, and importantly, suffering the loss of a piece of himself. To be sure, war destroyed the countryside beauty and art before it; it "robbed us of very much we had loved." That is horrible, but we know war does that. But, as he puts it, "it also *shattered our pride . . . our admiration . . . our hopes. . . .*"[4] It "tarnished" our sense of science's loftiness; it revealed severe limits on what the "noblest minds" can teach. I used to read this without pause; now, I find it surprising and in need of explanation. It is one thing to be grief-stricken or depressed or enraged by the destruction of great art and great beauty. It is quite another thing to have "our" pride, admiration, and hopes shattered.

Of course, Freud's "our" need not include us. He is inviting his intended or expected readers to recognize something similar in themselves. The important point is that Freud is talking about a psychic phenomenon—shattered pride—that he takes to be a shared and significant response to the destruction of war, and one that can be recognized as such by those who are suffering from it. We contemporary readers may not find ourselves in this particular use of the first-person plural, but we can nevertheless learn from it.

There is something personal here: not just that Freud is personally affected, but that this *somehow has to do with who he is.* Freud is ashamed. He says that war "showed us how ephemeral were many things *that we had regarded as changeless.*" But that alone cannot explain shattered pride. It must have been that *he himself*—and his intended readers—were somehow invested, not just in these cultural achievements but in their being eternal or "changeless." The narcissism of this group seems to have been entangled in an illusion that civilization is itself *an endless journey*—a long trip in a civilizing direction, one that moves toward peace and mutual understanding, in which increased knowledge is a civilizing force, and reason and creative art promote social and psychic harmony. On this image, civilization opens indefinitely into the future and in the direction of the good. It is in this context that we can understand what Freud means by war tarnishing the "lofty impartiality" of our science. War does not show scientific results false, but it does destroy the illusion that science facilitates peaceful progress for all, and it shows how science is used to destroy civilization. Freud thus admits to a twofold illusion: first, that civilization is an endless progressive journey; second, that by participating in that journey one can take pride *in oneself* because one thereby partakes, as best one can, in something eternal and good. Disillusion thus comes as a blow to Freud's sense of self. Shattered pride means that he was implicated in the illusion—not simply because he participated in it but because he *identified* with it.

Here is the wishful kernel that, until this blow of recognition, has been part of Freud's self-conception: that if one hitches oneself up to civilization's long trip, one can thereby partake of eternity. Only thus could *"our pride"* be shattered in the recognition that eternity does not come with the bargain. There is also room for embarrassment in recognizing one's complicity in maintaining the illusion. After all, European culture had been riven by wars for thousands of years; works of art and monuments to culture have been destroyed again and again through the ages. How could it be that over and over again, there arises the comforting belief that we have somehow arrived at a turning point, where civilization at last gains the upper hand over destructiveness? Of course, the "we" of Freud and his intended readers does not coincide with we current readers. And yet, I am reminded of a more recent time, just after the fall of the Berlin Wall, when Francis Fukiyama published *The End of History and the Last Man*—to great popular acclaim in magazines and journals—that yet again claimed we are at such a culminating point in history. There is a repetition here—and in the midst of the coronavirus pandemic it is a good time to take another look at it.

While the transience of world structures and civilizational achievements may be on our minds, what may be haunting our musings is the *actual transience* in the here and now of our own psychic well-being. We may anticipate mourning the end of the world but be confused about how to acknowledge a lost or damaged part of ourselves. There is, then, something to be gained by reading Freud as *working through* this very problem. If, as I have suggested, we begin toward the end of the essay with Freud's shattered pride and admiration—the tarnished sense of the nobility of science with which he had identified, all in response to world catastrophe—we can then return to the main body of the essay and read it as an active attempt at intrapsychic mourning and repair.

The Summer Walk

Let us now go back to the beginning of Freud's essay:

> Not long ago I went on a summer walk through a smiling
> countryside in the company of a taciturn friend and of a

young but already famous poet. The poet admired the beauty of the scene around us but felt no joy in it. He was disturbed by the thought that all this beauty was fated to extinction, that it would vanish when winter came, like all human beauty and splendor that men have created or may create. All that he would otherwise have loved and admired seemed to him to be shorn of its worth by the transience which was its doom."[5]

It is all but certain that this summer walk never occurred.[6] The Editors of the *Standard Edition* tell us that Freud went on vacation in the Dolomites in August 1913, but they know nothing of the poet or friend. Scholars have pointed out that Freud did meet a famous poet a month later, in September, but that meeting took place *in a city*, in Munich, and in the midst of a fraught and frenetic Congress of the International Psychoanalytic Association. This was an occasion of the break between Freud and his hoped-for protégé Carl Jung. To put it mildly, Freud had a lot on his mind. And there was no smiling countryside or other natural scene to admire. Lou Andreas-Salomé wrote in her journal that she was able to introduce her friend Freud to her friend and lover Rainer Maria Rilke: "I was delighted to bring Rainer to Freud, they liked each other, and we stayed together that evening until late at night."[7] Matthew von Unwerth says in his book *Freud's Requiem:* "The meeting was not, in all likelihood, *a trois,* but in the company of other psychoanalysts attending the Congress, or perhaps with friends of Rilke and Lou. Their intimate conversation might have just as easily been shouted over laughter at a cramped corner table as passed in whispers to circumvent the crowding noise."[8] On the basis of this Munich meeting, scholars have suggested that Rilke must be the famous young poet and Andreas-Salomé the taciturn young friend. One scholarly strategy has been to deploy literary and historical research to figure out what that conversation might have been. This has led to fascinating insights, and no doubt more are forthcoming. But in this essay, I want to take a different tack.

Basically, for the purpose of this interpretation, I suggest we forget about Rilke and Andreas-Salomé. And we abandon the idea that there was *any meeting*—whether in the Dolomites or in Munich—that was *the* meeting we need to get clear about. Rather than follow Freud's narrative, which is fiction, I suggest we begin with the psychic devastation recorded near the end of the essay. We should look to the beginning as a retrospective attempt to contain the anxiety. The encounter with Rilke may well have served as an inspiration for Freud's imagination (what he would call a day residue). But the "Young Poet" is better understood not as corresponding to any real figure in the external world but rather as a figment of Freud's imagination. And, importantly, this *figment* of Freud's imagination is also a *fragment* of his imagination. The Young Poet lacks nuance or complexity. From *this* perspective, it is a mistake to try to fill out the picture with a more textured sense of who this poet was or what the conversation might have been. As a figure in Freud's *inner* world, it is the caricature that matters. The "conversation" that interests us here is not any real-life conversation that went on in the social world; rather, it is the "conversation" of intrapsychic dynamics of figures of the imagination. (Psychoanalysts sometimes call these internal figures "part objects" because they tend to lack nuance. They are, for instance, all good or all bad.) In the case we are considering, the "conversation" is an attempt to repair psychic damage of living through world catastrophe.

The fact is that the purported argument between the Poet and Freud, *if taken at face value,* is a shambles. The Poet comes across as immature and arrogant, taking a dramatic stance for the sake of the drama. It is more like a debating position.

For his part, the Freud of the vignette, the "I," is an equally one-sided figure on the other side: "But I did dispute the pessimistic poet's view that transience of what is beautiful involves any loss in its worth. *On the contrary, increase!* Transience value is scarcity value in time. Limitation of the possibility of enjoyment raises the value of the enjoyment. It was incomprehensible I declared, that the thought of transience of beauty should interfere with our joy in it."[9] Incomprehensible? To be sure, we do have relationships in which we poignantly grasp their vulnerability, transience, and overall finiteness. That may well contribute to our sense of their preciousness. But ask anyone who has declined to enter a relationship because they did not think it would last. It is difficult to see how Freud's enthusiasm for transience—"On the contrary, increase!"—could begin to persuade. Later in the essay, Freud acknowledges the terrible pain of loss, but the "I" who appears *in this conversation* with the Poet is a thoroughly unambivalent figure. This is not a thoughtful engagement between two serious people about the meaning of transience in human life; rather, it is a polarized standoff between caricatured figures in Freud's imagination. Neither stance is nuanced nor insightful about the position of the other. They are simply opposites set over against each other. The Poet is characterized by his refusal to take joy in transient beauty. The "Freud" of the debate is the opposite: taken up with the thought that the transience of beauty is the source and justification of joy.

This polarized standoff makes perfect sense if one thinks of it as the *aftermath* of the disillusionment that Freud describes himself as having undergone. Freud has just lost an organizing fantasy of his life: the image of himself as participating in civilization's long trip and *thereby* partaking of eternity. He is living with a damaged ego ideal. What emerges is a divided structure—a "debate" in which no matter which side you are on, you do not rely on the fantasy of civilization partaking of eternity.

Note, too, that *if* the underlying kernel of anxiety is about the fragility of civilization, then the whole scene of a nature walk is a projection outward to a place most unlikely to raise the issues genuinely at stake. Put yourself in the mindset of a European intellectual at the beginning of World War I and ask yourself: Is there anything in the world that seems more permanent, more intransient, more unlikely to be harmed by human destructiveness than the Dolomite Mountains? If, by contrast, Freud had set his conversation at a café in Munich, the conversationalists might well be led to wonder whether these precious café conversations might go out of existence, whether indeed cities might survive. (These are not unlike questions we are asking ourselves now.) And the Poet's explicit concern, if taken at face value, is close to preposterous. He is reported to be "disturbed by the thought that *all this beauty* was fated to extinction"; but what he means is "that it would vanish *when winter came.*" In short, he is talking about *the lilies of the field* in a high-altitude Dolomite meadow.[10] True, *those* lilies will die come winter, but is there any stronger image of permanence than the eternal cycle of nature in which the lilies "return" each spring?

Revolt Against Mourning

Freud gives a diagnosis of what is going on with the Poet and his friend:

> These considerations appeared to me incontestable; but I noticed that I had made no impression either upon the poet or upon my friend. My failure led me to infer that some powerful

emotional factor was at work which was disturbing their judgment, and I believed later I discovered what it was. What spoilt their enjoyment must have been a revolt in their minds against mourning. The idea that all this beauty was transient was giving these two sensitive minds a foretaste of mourning over its decease; and since the mind instinctively recoils from anything that is painful, they felt their enjoyment of beauty interfered with by thoughts of its transience.[11]

This is a justly famous diagnosis. The *revolt in their minds against mourning* picks out a strategic but ultimately irrational mental activity that we would now call an attack on linking: the mind anticipates the pain of mourning in the future over a loss and rushes forward in the present to attack the formation of any attachment that would make one vulnerable to loss.[12]

So far, so good. But let us think again about where the revolt in the mind against mourning is located. Purportedly, it is *over there* in the mind of the Poet. But let us take a step back and take in the whole scene: we have one figure—the Poet—who refuses to take pleasure in beauty so as to avoid the pain of mourning in the future, and we have another figure—the "author" or "Freud"—who *in this scene* is an unambivalent advocate for transience. And thus, willingness to acknowledge the ambivalence and accept the pain of mourning has—in this scene—been left out. That gives us reason to peek backstage—not to Freud *as depicted in this scene* but rather to Freud the author who, in depicting this scene, is leaving ambivalence out. This is a Freud who, as we are exploring, declared damage to his own ego (shattered pride and admiration) in the context of world catastrophe. This damaged inner world depended on the illusion of the long trip: that one could participate in immortality (somehow) by identifying with civilization and its progress.

The depicted scene—the standoff between Poet and "Freud"—is, from this perspective, a first effort to restore ideals. It is a picture of omnipotent battle: purportedly, the Poet will never have to suffer due to his high-principled strategy; and for the Freud of this scene, transience is an unambivalent measure of increase in value. A battle of ideals is in play, but it is manic and fractured. However, this is an early stage in an attempted restoration.

Intrapsychic Repair

Freud turns to mourning, the phenomenon he thinks the Poet is guarding himself against. "Mourning over the loss of something that we have loved or admired seems so natural to the layman that he regards it as self-evident. But *to psychologists, mourning is a great riddle*—one of those phenomena that cannot themselves be explained but to which other obscurities can be traced back."[13] This purported contrast between "laymen" (or ordinary people) and psychologists seems more like a fantasy of a social division than the real thing.[14] For one thing, there is an important difference between *grief coming* naturally to us on the death of a loved one and *mourning seeming* natural to us. The former seems true, the latter questionable. Mourning typically involves attempting to join a cultural ritual that puts itself forward as an adequate manner of response to the death of a loved one. For some, these rituals may be satisfying; for others, there may be moments of alienation; for others, they may not work at all. The idea that there is a class of "ordinary people" for whom mourning seems so natural does not stand up to reflective scrutiny.

Let us instead entertain the thought that the purported social division that Freud describes is a projection outward onto society of a struggle going on *within* the human soul or psyche—a struggle that an individual human being such as Freud (or his readers) could experience. The struggle is to restore a damaged ego ideal in the midst of world catastrophe. How does one restore a sense of pride and admiration in relation to a world that is itself in turmoil? "Ordinary people," in this context, are the imaginary others in relation to whom one can feel pride as one identifies with the inspiring image of the psychologist.

Who are the "psychologists"? I am struck that Freud uses the word "psychologist" rather than "psychoanalyst."[15] Freud may have intended to use it simply as a synonym, but the term has an expansive life. Officially, it refers to a socially recognized class of professionals, but the term opens out to a broader sense: to humans who, in response to a psychic shake-up, seek to understand and give an account of what that shake-up is—that is, to give a *logos of the psyche*. In short, the Psychologist is someone who can transform the pain of mourning into a riddle of what mourning is all about. In the figure of the Psychologist, Freud, in my opinion, is trying to build up an image he can admire, take pride in, and *identify with*. He is constructing a more robust ego ideal.

Freud has taught us that our imaginary figures tend to be dense with condensations. I suggest there are at least four figures are condensed into the image of the Psychologist: *Socratic, scientist, post-Oedipus,* and *humanist.* This condensation lends unusual robustness to the ego ideal. Let me say a word about each.

- Socratic: The Psychologist knows that he does not know. For him, mourning is a "great riddle." This is not a figure who can be brought down by pretending to a knowledge that he does not have.
- Scientist: Knowing that one has a riddle sustains open-ended curiosity about how things are.

- Post-Oedipus: For Oedipus, having a "great riddle" meant only one thing: find a solution! First time, it seemed like a triumph; second time, it was his undoing. By contrast, the Psychologist's "great riddle"—mourning—is "one of those phenomena *which cannot themselves be explained* but to which other obscurities can be traced back." Mourning is not the kind of riddle *we solve*. It is a riddle we learn to live with. We live with it well by learning how to trace other phenomena back to it.
- Humanist: One comes back to the human condition again and again *not* in the sense of explaining the riddle but rather in trying to understand ourselves as creatures constituted by it. This is the spirit of the humanities.

The Psychologist

Freud's "great riddle" concerns the pain that is internal to our love life: that in falling in love with another we become *attached* to them, and we thereby make ourselves vulnerable to their vulnerabilities—in this case, to their being transient beings. Should they die, we do not *just* move on to someone else; we *suffer their loss*. As I argued in Chapter 1, it is this suffering that transforms what otherwise would be mere change into loss. And it thus turns us into historical beings in that we keep the past alive in emotion-laden, meaning-filled memories.

Freud is clear that we form attachments not only to other people but also to ideas and ideals, to nations and causes and peoples, to religious beings—God and angels and spirits—to cultural achievements and natural wonders and beauties. Through all our attachments, we make ourselves vulnerable to loss. Indeed, we inadvertently make ourselves doubly vulnerable. For as we form our attachments, we are liable, without quite noticing what we are doing, to *identify* with them—that is, to take *personal pride* in, say, the purportedly eternal achievements of civilization. Should there be disillusionment with the ideal, we not only suffer *that* loss, we also, as it were, are snuck up from behind and have to suffer the unexpected loss of a piece of ourselves.

"Such then," says Freud, "is mourning." He is speaking in the voice of the Psychologist, which, I believe, is the voice of a newly refurbished ideal, which is at the same time a refurbished *ego ideal*— one that is created in the very act of formulating the Psychologist's great riddle. This is itself an act of mourning: mourning the loss of a less robust ideal of civilization as an endless trip of progress. In short, Freud is *speaking from* his own loss and suffering. We readers are in some sense caught up in Freud's love affair—in this case, with the ideals with which to love and identify.

The English translation of this essay is "On Transience," and the preposition "on" suggests that the author takes himself to writing on a topic, transience, from a scientifically respectable distance. But the German title has no preposition. It is simply *Vergänglichkeit*. If I were to take a translator's liberty, I would not add a preposition but rather two punctuation marks: an exclamation point and a question mark—*Transience!?* The essay is as much an *expression* of our feelings of transience as a study of it.

As a native English speaker, I want to record a different valence I experience in the words *transience* and *change*. Change is impersonal. Change happens. It makes sense to us to talk about *mere* change. Transience signifies impermanence, but there is also the suggestion that our hearts are in it. Transience hints of loss. There is thus a wistfulness to *transience* that *change* does not have.

If we can experience this valence, then Freud's essay poses a new version of the chicken-or-egg question: Do we mourn because of the transience of the world? Or is the world transient because we mourn it? Without there being beings like us—with our capacity to love—would there only be change? It is not that we impose transience on a world or that transience is merely a human projection. Rather, transience manifests itself in a world full of lovers and lovables. Transience and mourning would seem to arise together.

Repetition

I am reading "On Transience" as *performance* of psychic repair in the midst of world catastrophe. As Freud concludes, he *returns to the original scene* of psychic loss, but now with a restored ego ideal:

> I believe that those who . . . seem ready to make a permanent renunciation because what was precious has proved not to be lasting, are simply in a state of mourning for what is lost. Mourning as we know, however painful it may be, comes to a spontaneous end. When it has renounced everything that has been lost, then it has consumed itself, and our libido is once more free (insofar as we are still young and active) to replace the lost objects by fresh ones equally or still more precious. *It is to be hoped that the same will be true of the losses caused by this war.* When once the mourning is over, it will be found that our high opinion of the riches of civilization has lost nothing from our discovery of their fragility. We shall build up again all that war has destroyed, and perhaps on firmer ground and more lastingly than before.[16]

Who are these people Freud diagnoses as mourning—those tempted to renounce civilization's achievements because of their fragility?

It must be Freud himself and his intended readers. Or rather, it is Freud as he described his *previous* condition—a moment ago, as it were—before performing the psychic repair expressed in this very essay. Indeed, Freud's own mourning comes to an end precisely in his diagnosis *of others* as being in mourning. And if readers can use this essay to make a similar journey—indeed, use this passage *as an interpretation*—they too may be able to emerge from their own mourning, now recognized as such.

At first, this conclusion can be disturbing. *Even mourning*, it seems, is transient. Freud's great riddle, as he presented it, is that we are creatures who mourn at all. But the other side of that riddle is that after some time we move on. Of course, mourning is not itself fickle: people's lives, personalities, memories, values, and commitments can be changed forever by the people with whom they fall in love and, indeed, by the causes with which they have come to identify. Freud is talking about mourning in the familiar sense of that term: the socially recognized period of withdrawal from what had been everyday forms of life. However, in a deeper, psychoanalytically informed sense of the term—one made possible by Freud's own meditations—mourning may continue on throughout a life and, indeed, constitute our humanity.[17]

But what does a return to life consist in *in the midst of world catastrophe*? Freud says, "It is to be hoped . . . ," and in those very words Freud is *expressing hope*.[18] He is doing this in the midst of the catastrophe. The war is not over. Yet, his words mark the *return* of hope. And this return of hope is his emerging from mourning: mourning the loss of the ideal of civilization as never-ending *progress*. War has destroyed that. For an Enlightenment atheist such as Freud, this is the secular equivalent of the death of God. Freud can no longer imagine himself as doing one's meaningful bit by participating in this image of eternity.

But then, how does one emerge from mourning? I want to claim that Freud here installs an ideal of *repetition* that he does not explicitly conceptualize as such. He expresses the hope that "we shall build up again all that war has destroyed." No one could mean that literally. We do not wish to bring back destroyed systems of injustice, exploitation, and evil. To that, we say *good riddance*. We are in fact hoping for transience . . . *of the bad and evil*. Freud expresses the hope of building back up again all *the good* that catastrophe has destroyed, but maybe in this next repetition, it will be even better. The words Freud uses are "perhaps on firmer ground and more lastingly than before." The hope acknowledges that we cannot be all that determinate about what we are hoping for.[19] The hope, then, is both ironic and at the same time earnest: *for a return . . . perhaps this time better!* This is what it is for Freud to emerge from mourning the destruction of civilization.

It might be surprising to see a positive conception of repetition in the writings of Freud. In his explicit writings on the topic, the concept of repetition has a negative aura. Repetition is the condition of neurotics, people failing to flourish. They unconsciously repeat conflicts over and over again.[20] It almost feels fated. There is even an intimation of eternity—that the repetition of the unhappy-making same is *all there is*. This negative conception of repetition is contrasted with positive conceptions of *remembering* and *working through*.

Freud does not formulate a positive conception of repetition *named as such*, but it is there to be found in his conception of mourning. Of course, the world may overwhelm us, it may destroy us, it may eliminate any chance of happiness or psychic well-being, it may make us miserable for life. But *if it does not*, then it is characteristic of us that we respond to loss with pain and suffering but then tend in the direction of returning to life. Like and yet so unlike the lilies, it is *we* who return transformed by painful loss and active imagination. The return is itself an expression of hope. We may not be able to say what we are hoping for, but in the broadest and most indeterminate sense, hope hopes for the good. So, what we have here is a *return of hope, which is itself a hope for a return of the good.* From Freud's point of view, this is who we are when we are doing well.

It seems to me now that Freud, writing in his time of world catastrophe, was struggling with issues of legitimacy in imaginative life. In particular, he saw that longings for immortality could no longer be gratified via a fantasy of civilization's long trip. The substitute ideal—repetition—is admittedly more fragile: we are not guaranteed that our species is eternal or that a habitable world will last. Still, this acknowledgment can open room for more sustainable forms of fantasy, for a good-enough imaginative world. There is an intimation of eternity in repetition: (for as long as we endure) we shall tend in the direction of returning with hope, a hope for the return of the good. It seems to me that there is further hope to be gleaned from the recognition of the durability of hope (even in the midst of our fragility) that is internal to the human.

But repetition in this positive sense has been less explored in the psychoanalytic tradition than the pathological forms. The only thinker I know of who has thought deeply about repetition in this "good sense" is Søren Kierkegaard, but for him, repetition was available only through Christian faith.[21] A question thus opens up for psychoanalysts and philosophers whether a plausible conception of healthy repetition can be formulated in such a way as to be available to a wide range of people and their forms of living. It remains important unfinished business in the human understanding of the human to comprehend the scope, limits, and possibilities of repetition in this "good sense." Perhaps the pandemic has opened up some opportunities for understanding.

3

Exemplars and the End of the World

Priam, The Last King of Troy

It is difficult not to be preoccupied with climate change and ecological catastrophe, threats to the democratic political order, as well as the menace of pandemic. These threats are real, and we shall need to think hard and well in the hope of finding ways to alleviate them. It is no surprise, then, that our imaginations should come alive. In health, we imagine alternative possibilities. Our imaginations open up the future, recreate the past, and enliven the present. These are virtues, or excellences, of imagination. But we also know that imagination can get in our way, distort our vision, and insist that falsehoods are true. When it comes to imagination, there is such a thing as ill health. So, what I am concerned with are real threats to the imagination as we face real threats coming from the world. I have been arguing that our concerns with the *end* of the world in the sense of catastrophe has interfered with our sense of the *end* of the world in the sense of the ideals and values that in healthy times inform human life and give us a sense of what life is all about. There is a sense of disorientation—not only about the world but about ourselves: what to take pride in, what to admire or commit to with confidence. In Chapters 1 and 2, I have argued that a sense of what is fine, noble, and beautiful about human life can go missing.

It is in this context that I want to return to the last great Trojan king, Priam—that is, Priam as he makes an appearance at the beginning of Aristotle's *Nicomachean Ethics*. As is well known, it is Priam's fate to "rule" over the destruction of his own kingdom and to suffer the killing of his beloved son Hector and the desecration of his body. Priam then begs Achilles, his son's killer, for the body back. As Homer memorably has Priam say, "I have endured what no one on earth has ever done before—I put to my lips the hands of the man who killed my son."[1] It is astonishing that Aristotle, his students, and we now, millennia later, can all draw on the same literary figure, King Priam, as he is depicted in Homer's *Iliad*. For Aristotle, Priam is the exemplar of the noble person of high standing who had to suffer world catastrophe. Before the pandemic, I read this as an example of the tragic hero, once riding so high then brought so low by fate, but maintaining his dignity through it all. In short, I read it as a familiar trope. Now, I read Aristotle as making an important point about the dynamic interplay between happiness and the *kalon* in human life.

For Aristotle, each of the species has its distinctive form of flourishing, but our form is on a different level altogether. Our form of flourishing is happiness (or *eudaimonia*), and *therefore* Aristotle says, "*it makes perfect sense* that we do not say that an ox, a horse or any other animal whatsoever is happy."[2] The reason he gives is that they have no capacity to participate in *kalon* activities—for they are insensitive to *the fine, the noble, the beautiful* as such. The Greek term that I gloss as "participate" is more literally construed as *act so as to be in community with.*[3] This, Aristotle says, is the key to our happiness: the active exercise of our ability to recognize and delight in, to be amazed by, to want to emulate, and to imitate those exemplars of the *kalon* that we experience in life, as well as our success, through practice, in internalizing and identifying with the *kalon* so that, having acquired human virtue or excellence, we, in our life activities, shine forth with the *kalon* ourselves. This is more than a necessary condition of our happiness (as, for example, some external goods are needed). Appropriate responsiveness to, internalization of, and active participation in the *kalon* is what our happiness consists in.

And yet, although we can be stripped of our happiness by extreme misfortune—as Priam was—Aristotle insists that nothing— *nothing at all that the external world can throw our way*—can altogether alienate us from the *kalon* once we have internalized it, that is, become virtuous. Terrible reversals of fortune may spoil such a person's "blessedness," but even in such cases, his "nobility shines through."[4] That is why, Aristotle thinks, that while a virtuous person is vulnerable, in extreme circumstances, to unhappiness, he could never become wretched or perform base actions.[5] So, here in a nutshell is the complex relation between happiness and the *kalon:* although achieving the *kalon* is constitutive of our happiness, and although extreme misfortune—such as world catastrophe—can destroy our happiness, *once the kalon has been achieved, nothing can completely destroy it in us. A kernel remains that is inalienable.* That is Aristotle's teaching.

Aristotle's account of Priam is, of course, in plain view, but I do not think the idea of an inalienable kernel of the *kalon* has got the attention it deserves in contemporary Aristotelian-inspired approaches to ethics because they tend to focus on the resilience of the virtuous person: his or her ability to sustain happiness across a wide range of worldly circumstances. It is assumed that worldly circumstances will be within a familiar range. But when the prospect of world catastrophe comes near, as it has done for us with threats of ecological or virus-induced destruction, the issue of *what if?* becomes more salient.

It is in this context that Aristotle's rhetorical strategy comes more clearly into view. Aristotle says his lectures are intended to make a practical difference: to help his audience or readers on their journey to virtue and the good. Thus, his aim with Priam as exemplar is not as it were a specimen for a *theoretical* examination of the high brought low. It is meant to be of practical benefit to those who are learning from Aristotle: his actual audience or those readers of the *Nicomachean Ethics* who are actually using the book as Aristotle intended it should be used. Aristotle's intended audience are people who are very much en route to virtue, that is, human excellence, or, even better, those who have achieved virtue and are looking to consolidate it further by better understanding what it is. These are people who, *to some extent,* perhaps just a little, have already experienced the joy and delight and wonder of the *kalon*—as they have seen it in others—and have taken steps, through practice and emulation, to internalize it in themselves. Thus, they ought to be able to experience the *kalon*—at least up to a certain point—*from the inside.*

So, in the case we are considering, Aristotle the teacher is installing the exemplar Priam in his students, along with a certain way of *taking up* Priam in thought, a certain way of conceiving him, as they themselves consider the virtuous life, and the relation of happiness and the *kalon*. Students thus acquire the capacity *to return* to Priam again and again in thought and imagination throughout the course of their lives. Priam was an available cultural figure for Aristotle and his students, and he remains so for us. He may have been based on an actual character; he may have been a Homeric creation. Either way, Priam is a familiar figure who, as it were, rests in our imaginations and whom we can easily call to mind. (This is what Aristotle would call a capacity or power of our minds.) Now, when we do call Priam to mind, our imaginations come alive, experiencing Priam in his exemplarity. So, instead of continuing to focus on what is going on in Priam, let us focus on what ought to be going on in Aristotle's audience.

Normally, when we study Aristotle, we concentrate on his doctrines. Here, I would like us to shift our attention to the manner of his teaching. And let us imagine that we are part of Aristotle's intended audience. Aristotle's teaching at this point triggers the experience of Priam in thought and imagination. We imagine the famous scenes from Homer's *Iliad:* his kindness to Helen, despite the disaster she and Paris have caused; his dignity, even when having to beg Achilles for the corpse of his son. We imagine what a virtuous person might look like when living through extraordinary misfortune, and with Aristotle's help, we see the *kalon* shining through. What I want to suggest is that Aristotle is not just teaching us something *about* Priam, *he is also instilling a capacity to invoke Priam as an exemplar* as a means of building confidence *here and now* in our own emerging powers with the *kalon*. There is something about imagining the inalienability of the *kalon* that *rings true* and, in this way, builds confidence *in the present* in the robustness of the *kalon*. I am interested in this experience of persuasiveness, and I want to consider what it consists in.

Looking for the Right Kind of Exemplar

We are looking for an exemplar who can instill confidence in this kernel of inalienability of the *kalon*. And we would like to know how that works when it does work. Here, I am indebted to the work of Linda Zagzebski on exemplars in moral theory, though, given my interests, I am going to move in a different direction. She makes the important point that "we are often more certain of the identities of exemplars that we are of any conceptual foundation . . . we are more certain that Confucius, Jesus and Socrates are admirable than we are of claims about the good of pleasure, or what human flourishing is. . . . In fact," she continues, ". . . we are more certain *that* they are admirable than we are of *what* is admirable about them."[6] There is a crucially important insight here—that we can be *grabbed* by the beauty, by the *kalon*, of an exemplar before we understand in any detail what it is that is grabbing us. But Zagzebski's paradigms—Jesus, Confucius, Socrates—cloud this insight. Jesus, for example, is introduced to us typically through a cultural vehicle, the Christian Bible. The Gospels tell us a remarkable amount about *what it is* that makes Jesus so admirable. For many whose introduction to Jesus occurred in the interpretively rich context of Sunday school—hearing stories, singing hymns, listening to sermons—the route of influence is the opposite that Zagzebski describes: they moved from being impressed with *what* Jesus accomplished and, in particular, *what he taught* to being struck with admiration *for him*.

There is another problem. As Kierkegaard poignantly showed us, cultural vehicles can be put to the opposite use for which they are intended. Kierkegaard tried to get his neighbors to see that the "Christianity" they were living was a sham. Though he may have used the Bible to work his way back to Jesus as exemplar, he also

saw that in its general deployment in mid-nineteenth-century Den-
mark, the Christian Bible was used *to tranquilize* the population
into accepting a watered-down and dangerously misleading version of Christianity. Kierkegaard called Christendom—that is, the
contemporary cultural formation of Christianity—a "*dreadful* illusion." Part of what he meant was that one could talk all one
wanted about Jesus as an exemplar, of being struck by admiration
by him, of wanting to learn, imitate, and emulate him; one could
quote Bible passages and listen to or give sermons—and *all of it*
would be contained by, indeed would even reinforce the illusion.
In such a case, the invocation of the exemplar *would keep us at a
distance* from any experience of the exemplar.

It is beyond my competence to explain the decline in a culture's
ability to transmit the exemplarity of an exemplar. But the mere
fact that there can be such a decline gives us an important clue.
By the time of Kierkegaard's "Christendom," however it came
about, there was a culture of priests and preachers, of professors
and Sunday school teachers and commentators and journalists who
were failing at their tasks to bring the exemplar to life for the larger
community. That is, there was a widespread degeneration in the *local
exemplars:* the group of people whom the larger community expected to pass on to them what they needed to know—a group with
whom the community was more or less in direct contact—lost their
own ability to make the exemplarity of great exemplar—in this
case, Jesus—vivid. Their sermons and books and articles—the
examples they set—had a deadening effect that was not recognized as such.

This points us toward a priority in local exemplars: *the first responders,* as it were, to our need for the experience of something
"higher," "noble," "beautiful"—needs of spirit that I have been
calling a need for the *kalon.*[7] So, there is reason to look at the local

exemplar. Our question here is not what is going wrong when things break down, but rather what is going right when a local exemplar succeeds in exemplifying to his local audience. What does this elementary case of exemplarity look like?

A Local Hero

In the autumn of fourth grade, when I was ten years old, I swore on the playground. Although I vividly remember what followed, I cannot directly remember what I said. The class was at recess in late morning, it was a gray day, and I am pretty confident I said, "Goddammit." This is where my memory clicks in. A classmate overheard me, was upset, and ran over to tell the teacher. Mr. McMahon turned around, and he started walking toward me. He was wearing a trench coat, belted in the middle. His hair was in a crew cut, common among men at that time. He might have been a police detective in a television show. He came over, looked me in the eyes, and said in a low, calm voice: "We do not use profane language on the playground." He then turned around and walked away. That was it.

I have been thinking of this moment, on and off, ever since, and it has come back to me now as I try to think about confidence in the *kalon*. I would like to take a close look at the exemplarity of Mr. McMahon and ask what it consists in. Mr. McMahon's direct communication (as Kierkegaard would put it) was that I was not supposed to swear, and I certainly got that message. But I am here concerned not so much with his direct teaching as with what he *exemplified* (what Kierkegaard would call his *indirect* communication). I shall isolate and discuss five moments: *the enigmatic nugget internal to understanding, generosity of interpretation, nonretaliation, the persuasive power of reality,* and *protecting the playground.*

First, the enigmatic nugget. I had never heard the word "profane" before. I knew that he was telling me not to use bad words
on the playground. I knew he was going to tell me *that* before he
opened his mouth. But in the midst of his utterance, he enclosed
an enigmatic nugget: What was he telling me not to do? What is
a *profane* word? Something important was being said, it was being
said *to me,* and I did not know what it was, even though in some
sense I did. One might think I could solve the problem of what
"profane" meant by looking it up in the dictionary. I tried that. But
that turned out to be the beginning not the end of my inquiry. This
inquiry has moved in two directions. First, what did Mr. McMahon
mean when he used that word? Second, what does *profane* mean
anyway? These questions have become lifetime companions. It is
not that there are no answers; it is rather that the answers never
close the book on the questions. *Profane* is one side of a fundamental division, with *sacred* on the other side. Of course, the original home of this division is religious. But even within a secular
context, one can glimpse, however obscurely, an important divide:
over there, on the other side is something special and good, while
the profane is that which gets in the way and even spoils. But however clear one gets on this division and its cultural history, there is
always an enigmatic sense that there is more to learn.

This shows us something important about the exemplar–
recipient dyad. Mr. McMahon was a real figure who, decades ago,
made an impression on me. At some point, he left the playground
and went on to live his own life, and I left fourth grade to live mine.
Still, in some sense, he also took up residence in my imagination.
Not only can I call him to mind, but "he" can come alive in my
mind, as it were, of "his" own accord. He then continues to exert an
exemplary influence. And the continuing activity of the exemplar is
due, at least in part, to what I have been calling the "enigmatic

nugget." His utterance of the word "profane" became an intriguing grain of sand inside my imagination.

In recent years, I have imagined Mr. McMahon in that moment after he spoke to me, when he turned around to go back to where he had been. What was he thinking? Perhaps nothing. Or that it will be lunch time soon. But I have also imagined him smiling to himself, indiscernible to the outside world, and thinking, "*I've given that little fellow something to think about for the rest of his life.*"

I shall treat the next two features of local exemplars, *generosity of interpretation* and *nonretaliation,* together. If I had simply received a standard punishment, I suspect I would have forgotten about this moment long ago. But not only was Mr. McMahon using this strange word "profane," it was in a context in which I was not going to get punished. That was surprising enough. But even more so, it was as though punishment was not what this encounter was about *at all.* But then, what was it about? Socrates famously said that philosophy begins in wonder. This for me was a wondrous moment. Mr. McMahon saw me as someone for whom this "simple" statement was sufficient—this was his interpretive generosity.

But the generosity was uncannily apt. As Kierkegaard pointed out, Adam could not have understood what God was telling him not to do because he had not yet eaten from the tree of knowledge of good and evil.[8] Adam did not act *because* he was sinful; it was in the act that he sinned. I had heard the expression "Goddammit" circulating around my house, in the background, as my mother and father argued. So, I was in an Adam-like position. I had an intuition that this expression was used to express negative feelings, but I did not know what it meant. What I had was a possibility: a possibility for imitating my parents. But I did not understand *what* I had said until after I had committed the act. So, not only did I not understand what "profane" meant, I did not understand what I had said to provoke it. Nevertheless, *I had done it.* How does a teacher respond to this childish mixture of innocence and guilt?

I think this was a moment of creativity. Our drama did not have to play out according to a fixed pattern. Mr. McMahon saw me as a person I had not yet become: a person who needed no more than those words he spoke. And in his saying, I took up that possibility. I think this is the nub of my gratitude: not just that I did not get punished or humiliated—that would have provoked relief—but that there was something both comprehending and gracious in Mr. McMahon's attitude.

As for nonretaliation, it has become a life lesson: retribution in the name of justice rarely restores harmony. Nonretaliation is a centrally important trait both in a teacher and in a psychoanalyst. But in terms of understanding the role of an exemplar, there are two points. First, I do not think I could have learned the lesson via direct communication, by someone telling me that retaliation is bad. It had to be via exemplification: I needed to be on the receiving end. Second, the "power of the exemplar" lies not so much in the exemplar per se but in a dyad that stretches over space and time that includes the exemplar and the person who was on the "receiving end" of the exemplifying experience. The dyad instantiates *a structure of repetition* that I shall elucidate. On my side of the dyad, time and again, I am called back to nonretaliation as a way to be—and it has the structure of repetition I outlined in Chapter 2: the return of the good again—*only this time perhaps better!* It is through this repetition that nonretaliation has become established in me as an ego ideal. Not *quite* me: nonretaliation is not effortless at my core. But me in the sense that nonretaliation is established as an ideal, project and task. This life task, set up in repetition, remains somehow tied to the exemplar. I want to claim not only that I am strengthened by this structure of repetition, but also that the persuasive power of reality is enlivened. I shall try to make clear what I mean.

The Persuasive Power of Reality

Actuality demonstrates possibility. This is an important feature of exemplars that has not received the attention it deserves. Zagzebski says that "Exemplars are not just good, they are supremely excellent . . . supremely admirable. . . ."[9] I am not sure what this means, and I do not in any want to detract from the experiences of those who feel they have been influenced by exemplars of supreme excellence. But speaking in the context of my experience with a *local exemplar*, what mattered was not his supreme excellence, but rather the reality of the encounter. I know he was remarkable in that moment—and in several others—but it is precisely because of his reality that there is much about Mr. McMahon that I do not know and could not hope to know. That's what real experiences are usually like: much that happens is beyond one's ken. But ironically, all this not knowing adds to rather than subtracts from my confidence in what I do know. All the aspects of not knowing are part of what it is to experience something real.

Zagzebski says that "fictional exemplars are just as important" as real people. "One of the advantages of a fictional exemplar is that we get to see them in circumstances in which we would not be able to observe in real life, and we can have a window into their consciousnesses in a way that we rarely can do with actual people. What exemplars do for us and our moral conceptions is largely irrelevant to their actual existence."[10] I agree that fictional exemplars can be important to us, but there is a difference in how they come to matter. People are inspired by literary figures such as Dorothea Brooke or Pierre Bezukhov. Such characters are persuasive because of the insight and mastery of their authors. They may stimulate our imaginations in all sorts of directions, and that matters greatly. But our sense of their plausibility and persuasiveness is not via direct experience of their actuality. There is something importantly different about grasping the exemplarity of a certain form of ethical behavior via its actual manifestation. One experiences a possibility via its actualization. And part of that experience is and must be knowing that, precisely because it is real, there is much about the actual exemplar that one does not know.

The experience of actuality shows us we are dealing with a real possibility, not just a wishful illusion of one. Of course, it is part of dealing with real-life circumstances that a widening context may change how things appear to us. An apparently good act can, over time and changing circumstances, come in retrospect to seem to have been manipulative. This too is part of what it is to be in "real life." But, again, it is precisely this hermeneutic openness—and one's awareness of it—that, in certain circumstances, can add to one's confidence in the reality of experience rather than detract from it. This again is because of the structure of repetition that gets set up in reaction (and relation) to the exemplar. Again and again, I have come back to the generosity of interpretation and of nonretaliation—as calls to me as a way to live—and those calls have established in me a special sense of the kernel of the *kalon* in Mr. McMahon. It is precisely because I do not need or want to be persuaded of his supreme excellence, because I have had long experience of changing interpretations over time, because of all the uncertainties that dealing with reality involves—*because of all of this,* not in spite of it—that I am confident there is an inalienable kernel here.

Protecting the Playground and the Fourfold
Structure of Exemplary Repetition

In his act, Mr. McMahon established himself as guardian of the playground. He excluded "profane" language from it, but he did not exclude me. The manner of his getting rid of that language was consonant with playground life. It was serious but also gentle, and as I look back, it might even have been playful.

The exemplar exemplifying is not a momentary act but is better understood as a complex structure of repetition and return. There are at least four levels. First, *in memory,* we return to the exemplar and the actual moment. Of course, imagination gets involved; there is room for distortion and outright mistakes. I shall get to that. But memory itself is an intentional capacity: directed onto people and past events. In my case, I am able to remember Mr. McMahon. I exercise a capacity to stay in touch with a certain aspect of reality, the past. Part of what it is for me to do my thing as a human being is to stay in touch with the past, my past, in some way or other.

Second, our imaginations become active, *again.* If exemplars are to play a role in our lives, they will do so by returning again and again in a recurring yet unfolding elaboration. The imaginative re-engagement counts as play. As we saw in Chapter 1 in the discussion of Winnicott, play is activity that, at the same time, constitutes *resting* from the everyday task of keeping subject and object distinct. The issue of whether it is *just* imagination or whether certain aspects are "real" recedes into the background. Of course, there are many uses of play and myriad ways to live with exemplars. But in terms of consolidating a sense of the *kalon,* play has a way of washing out the "impurities." So, when I go back to Mr. McMahon, I focus on his generosity of interpretation and nonretaliation. Who knows what else was going on with him at the time? They are lost in play. There is no doubt that the society we were both born into was in many ways unjust. Did he partake in gender or racial stereotypes that were rampant at the time? These are questions that might well arise, and to good effect, when we are thinking through the complexity and nuance of the past. But they need not arise in play. In play, the beauty of the exemplar is allowed to shine forth in some kind of isolation, without the surrounding complexities of the wider world.

There is also room for a touch of magic. One further memory of Mr. McMahon: at the beginning of the school year, he told the class that we would learn the multiplication tables by heart. Soon, he told us, we would know that seven times seven equals forty-nine, *just like that!* As he said that, he snapped his fingers. I looked on in amazement. How could that come to be? To this day, should I hear that seven times seven equals forty-nine, I still feel a special pleasure. It is due to the particularity of Mr. McMahon—with all of his contingencies—that the aspirations of nonretaliation and generosity of spirit go together in me, along with a tinge of confidence that someday it will be just like snapping my fingers and getting to forty-nine.

The third moment of repetition is the *return from play to everyday life.* Play is "resting" in the sense of *restorative:* we *return* from play energized and reanimated. Precisely because the return is a return *from the playground,* it should be a rested and creative return. In the case of the local exemplar, the sense of the actuality of the actual event is enlivened, and the motivations that the exemplarity stirs up reaffirmed. As I said, in play, the kernel of the *kalon* is isolated, but in returning from play, the reality of this moment is reaffirmed. In this sense, play is a nourishing activity for both inner and outer worlds.

The fourth and final moment of this repetition is the return of this threefold structure again and again throughout life. It is the ever-creative return of an ever-creative repetition. Søren Kierkegaard once wrote: "The dialectic of repetition is easy; for what is repeated has been, otherwise it could not be repeated, but precisely the fact that it has been gives to repetition the character of novelty."[11] The important point here is that not just any recurrence is a repetition. Event E happens at time t. Event E happens at $t + 1$. There is recurrence, but knowing only this much, we have no idea whether there is repetition or not. The events need to be linked *by repetition*—and in the case of our ethical life with exemplars, I have been trying to give the account of what this consists in. Within such repetition, there is a unity of sameness and novelty: once again, but this time new and maybe even better. So, consider *playgrounds are for playing*. The claim can be read as an empty formalism, a tautology. But introduced by a local exemplar, in this case Mr. McMahon, it has become a life lesson I have returned to again and again. There is unending novelty in the arising contemporary challenge—whether in a classroom or in a psychoanalytic situation or in the family or with friends—to facilitate play. In this way, *playgrounds are for playing* becomes an unending lesson: one can always learn more, always get better at it. And yet, these repetitions are linked together *by the repetition* and, in the repetition, linked to the exemplar. The unity and novelty of repetition lends unity and novelty to a life.

Revision of Freud

For Freud, *the compulsion to repeat* lies at the core of neurotic life. Within the psychoanalytic situation this shows up as *transference*, which is a projection onto the analyst of some ancient scene—for example of a past failure of the analysand with a parent. "Repetition" within the psychoanalytic framework is a hallmark of being stuck. But from the perspective we have been developing, Freud's "compulsion to repeat" is actually a *failure* to repeat. Neurotic transference is a *failed* repetition. The novelty of true repetition is shut down. And *failed* repetition is not one more species of repetition; it is a breakdown and foreclosure of it. This is not merely a matter of nomenclature—that Freud called one thing "repetition," and I am using the same word to name a different phenomenon. It is an issue of how we are to understand the relation between sickness and health.

The following claim is open to caveats, but overall, Freud's conception of science allowed him to think that he could give a rigorous account of a pathological condition as though it were an isolatable condition that could be considered in itself. The issue of *what health consisted in*—in relation to which this pathological condition counted as pathological—could be left in the background. From this perspective, there is no room to see neurotic repetition as a *failure* of repetition because one does not have a clear view of what repetition—that is, healthy repetition—consists in. But what we are in fact seeing in so-called neurotic repetition is a breakdown in repetition due to a failure to find a good way to live with local exemplars, often parents, relatives, siblings, or teachers—those important figures with whom we first engage in emotional and ethical life. Of course, there are many reasons for breakdown—which may include bad parenting and bad exemplars. But what has broken down is the capacity for novelty internal to the unity of healthy repetition.

So, properly understood, the aim of psychoanalytic technique is not to *overcome* repetition but to *restore* it. Ironically, Freud's technique (at least, as he elaborates it here) is beautifully suited to address the problem: "We render the compulsion [to repeat] harmless, indeed useful, by giving it the right to assert itself in a definite field. We admit it into the transference as a playground in which it is allowed to expand in almost complete freedom. . . . The transference thus creates an intermediate region between illness and real life through which the transition from one to the other is made."[12] The task is to *restore and sustain the playground* in which a person's life with exemplars can return in genuine repetition.

Return to Aristotle

Aristotle does not spend an enormous amount of time discussing the inner world of the virtuous person, but I think his conception of ethical life is in the spirit of repetition, as outlined in this chapter. The virtues are themselves structures of repetition. Take courage, for instance. For the courageous person, everything that comes her way comes back to the courageous thing to do in the circumstances. Of course, lots of life does not fit some cliché—for example standing fast in front of the enemy—but that is just it: the issues of salience, of what courage requires here and now, are never absent. And yet, insofar as circumstances vary, there is forever novelty in the unity of the courageous life lived courageously. Aristotle says that if you want to understand what the practically wise thing is to do in any set of circumstances, one must turn to the judgment of the practically wise person, the *phronimos.* That is because there is no formulaic rule or algorithm that can be applied *again.* Rather, we need repetition, and only the *phronimos,* the virtuous person, is able to *live that out*—as Aristotle would say, *strike the mean*—yet again.

But now, having worked through the role of local exemplars, it seems as if there is something missing in Aristotle's account of ethical education. He emphasizes that we are creatures who need to be inducted into ethical life via practices of habituation. But who is to do the habituating? At one level, this is obvious: it will be parents and teachers and other culturally appropriate figures. But how? It can look as though nothing is missing. How are the virtues acquired? By habituation? But then, how does habituation work? It seems to me that the answer must be by the exemplary work *of local exemplars.* Imagine a mean-spirited selfish adult insisting that a child share with a sibling, over and over again. It would not surprise us to learn that the child ends up habituated into a life of resentment and selfishness, not generosity. One needs the habituation process to have exemplarity built into it: that is the way to capture the child's imagination, with a glimpse of the *kalon* in those who are teaching them.

This is a key moment in the transmission of the virtues from one generation to the next. It is not only a missing step in Aristotle's account of the acquisition of the virtues; it is crucial to understanding how his ethical teaching can have the efficacy it is supposed to have. We who have the privilege of participating in great cultural institutions of learning certainly have the opportunity to witness *failures* of teaching. There is, at one end of the spectrum, the whiz-through survey of the history of philosophy, with students emerging having heard that the virtuous person "strikes the mean." At the other end of this spectrum, there is the serious *theoretical* study of Aristotle's ethical thought without it making the slightest difference in how the students live their lives. For Aristotle's ethical teaching to make the right kind of difference—that is, the difference Aristotle intended it to make, a *practical* difference—it needs to be introduced to students who have already been inducted into the virtues, at least up to a certain extent. It is intended as a completion and perfection of that process. That means, as we now see, the students need already to have had significant exposure to their own local exemplars.

So, to be a proper student of Aristotle's ethical teaching, one needs to have already installed in one's psyche the structure of repetition we have been examining—a structure that leads back to a local exemplar, exemplifying the virtues. This is the context in which Aristotle introduces Priam. Priam is, of course, already part of a shared cultural imaginary. Aristotle's casual references to him make it clear he assumes that his audience is already familiar with Priam. So, Priam enters our lives *again,* as a repetition, but this time he is to be put to a particular ethical use. He is mentioned in the context of Aristotle's *practical* teaching. So, it is reasonable to assume he is introduced to make us better. But how? By the proper exercise of our own imaginations. In effect, Aristotle is asking his audience *to imagine the end.* And unlike our contemporary imaginings of world catastrophes—which, as we saw in Chapters 1 and 2, have rattled our confidence in our lives with ideals and values— Aristotle expects this imaginary exercise to make his audience stronger.

It has puzzled some commentators how Aristotle's teaching could make a practical difference. Isn't he just adding a *theoretical* understanding of the good life that his audience is already living? The invocation of Priam shows that the development of self-conscious understanding in Aristotle's ethics involves more than the development of a theoretical grasp of what we already know.

Aristotle's invocation is a stimulus to the imagination. As imagination comes alive in play, the question of where Priam is located— Spread out throughout the culture? Over there in Troy long ago? A figment of Homer's imagination? A figure in my subjective life?—loses salience. We are, in effect, invited to participate in an act of imaginative consolidation. Priam is given an explicit exemplary meaning by Aristotle, but he is at the same time woven into a network of local exemplars, and they all, in turn, have been woven into a relation with Aristotle the teacher in the developing life of the student being taught. If all is going well in Aristotle's teaching, students already have a fairly well-established sense of ethical well-being: they have glimpsed and been attracted to the *kalon* not only by their experiences with exemplars, but also from their own internal sense of acting from virtue. They can feel something of the *kalon* in their own activity—and directly experience its pleasure and importance. The *kalon* is already embedded in their sense of self, albeit in a preliminary manner.

The point of Aristotle introducing Priam as an exemplar is not to give students instructions on how to behave should they suffer world catastrophe in the future, but rather to build a sense of resilience *in the present* with their emerging sense of the *kalon*. In effect, Aristotle is stimulating an imaginative exercise in his students. In imagination, Aristotle's students spend time with Priam, a figure who, when he was in *his* prime, was doing great but who later lost everything that made life valuable and meaningful. This is anticipatory mourning—a form of playing with the possibility of loss. If this imaginative exercise is to be part of ethical education, students must emerge from it with an increased sense of plausibility. For these students, already en route to a virtuous life, the sense of plausibility ought to come from it *fitting in* with their own experience—that is, with their experience of *their local exemplars* who have introduced them into the virtues. In this way, the imaginative exercise builds confidence that they have indeed touched on something inalienable in the *kalon*.

Mourning *or* Melancholia

In Chapters 1–3, I have been concerned with attempts to imagine the end of the world. And I have been inquiring into what counts as more or less healthy exercises of the imagination. As I have stressed, *even if the threats of world catastrophe* are real, and *even if our imaginations are stimulated by those very real threats,* that does not in itself make our imaginings healthy. But, then, what does imaginative health consist in? This is not an easy question to answer, but the inquiries have repeatedly led me back to basic insights Freud laid down in his paper, "Mourning and Melancholia," just over a century ago. In a way, it is odd that Freud's distinction should have such lasting power, since he was trying to give an account of a then-familiar diagnosis—"melancholia"—that is now, as such, gone with the wind. But his account was of such depth and generality that it, as it were, broke through the diagnosis and took on a life of its own. In "melancholia," Freud gives us a fundamental mode of human being, one of our basic ways of being attuned to the world. It has the structure of love and hate. As erotic and vulnerable creatures, one way we respond to loss or death or disappointment or the break-up of a significant relation, to ending or separation or betrayal, is with *furious identification.* Strange as it may seem, in fantasy, we "take in" the very thing that has let us down and then, as it were, berate ourselves for the loss. Or we leave it a bit vague who or where is the object of fury. As we saw in Chapter 1, "We will not be missed!" is a classic example of the fury being directed onto ourselves . . . *or maybe not.*

Mourning too is a response to loss but with a significant difference. The paradigm of mourning is of course over the death of a loved one. But again, the concept breaks open to include a pervasive aspect of the human condition: our ever-recurring need to deal with separation and loss. Mourning reveals itself as a basic mode of human being. In mourning, as with melancholia, there is identification. In fantasy, we "take in" the lost one but, in marked contrast with melancholia, in mourning, the imaginative playground is preserved. There may be anger at the departed loved one, but not so much as to destroy the playing field of repetition. Our imaginations come alive, going over our memories and feelings, our joys and disappointments and resentments, our sense of loss and, on occasion, our sense of the incredible specialness of it all. It is in this process that the exemplarity of the exemplar begins to shine forth. The other important difference about mourning is that it tends in the direction of a return to life. As Freud put it, mourning comes to a "spontaneous end." Thus, mourning is constitutive of the repetition that I have suggested characterizes human flourishing; melancholia is an angry attack on the possibility of repetition. They are two modes of living in a world that is not entirely up to us.

We are now living more than a century after Freud wrote his essay. I have been wondering what I would change about it, especially now that our imaginations are so taken up with the prospects of world catastrophe. Here is my suggestion of the smallest change that would make the biggest difference: that we change the "and" in "mourning and melancholia" to an "or." The "and" suggests the diagnostic position of the psychologist Freud, looking on these human conditions from a clinical distance. The "or" suggests that we are *in the midst of it:* we are confronted by different modes of being—that is, different ways *for us* to be—and it is not at all easy "from the inside" to tell just where we are or what to do. Mourning *or* melancholia is not a simple choice. It is not a matter of just deciding or exercising our will. As Freud (as well as Plato and Aristotle) taught us, much that goes on in our psychic formation eludes our conscious understanding and certainly our will. But that does not mean we cannot become active with respect to shaping our own lives and manners of being, that we cannot work in the direction of repetition. Precisely because we face such huge challenges to the continued existence of the world, we are simultaneously challenged to take seriously the healthy use of our imaginations.

4

When Meghan Married Harry
A Comment on the Humanities

I would like to take a look at a particular call of conscience that marks us as human. The example may at first look trivial, but the fact that a call can arise even here is important. And it will lead us to an insight about the meaning and value of the humanities. In her famous interview, Oprah Winfrey asked Meghan, Duchess of Sussex, "What are you most excited about in the new life?" Meghan answered, "I think just being able to live authentically." She gave as her prime example her wedding. "I was thinking about it—even at our wedding, you know, three days before our wedding, we got married . . ."

Oprah: Ah!
Meghan: No one knows that. But we called the Archbishop, and we just said, "Look, this thing, this spectacle is for the world, but we want our union between us." So, like, the

vows that we have framed in our room are just the two of
us in our backyard with the Archbishop of Canterbury, and
that was the piece that . . .

Harry: Just the three of us.

Oprah: Really?

Harry: Just the three of us.

Meghan: Just the three of us.[1]

Although she is a legendary interviewer, Oprah does not pick up
on what she has just been told. She responds: "The wedding was
the most perfect picture, you know, anybody's ever seen." But that
was precisely what Meghan was calling into question: whether that
"most perfect picture" really was a wedding.

Let us try to make Meghan's point of view more explicit. As a
social category (meaning the type of event or practice the social
sciences study), it seemed obvious that a wedding was about to take
place. But something troubled Meghan about that wedding, the
public occasion, being *her* wedding. As she told the Archbishop of
Canterbury, *that* event was a "spectacle . . . for the world," and here
she added the crucial *but:* "we want our union between us." That
is, the planned spectacle was not going to be the occasion in which
their union took place.

What we see here is a protest against the idea that the official
event was adequate to the seriousness of getting married. Where
does this niggle come from? It seems to come from the very idea
of marriage itself, at least as that idea is alive in Meghan's thought
and imagination. (Let me say at the beginning, that I have no interest in probing Meghan's individual psychology, inner world, or
deeper motivations. Nor will I discuss issues related to her character or the criticisms made of her in the media. I am only trying
to elaborate her self-conscious point of view.) Meghan wanted to

have a real wedding, not a sham. Her sense of her life as having meaning nudged her in the direction of *doing something different* than the planned public event. Looking back on it, she takes her doings to have been efficacious. She brought about a scene in the garden with Harry and the Archbishop of Canterbury that both she and Harry thought was adequate to their conception of marriage. She takes pleasure in their success. She called it living authentically and said *that* was what she was most excited about in her new life.

The official event on its own did not fit well into Meghan's conception of a meaningful life. Note the special sense of "meaningful" here. If Meghan had simply resigned herself to the demands of social custom, gone through the rituals with her heart in despairing fury, that would have been meaningful in some sense, but not in the sense Meghan sought and that we are tracking. In her actions, she expressed her conception of what it is to live a human life *well*. And here is the point: we have a conception of the human by which Meghan manifests her humanity precisely in striving to achieve her conception of what matters about living a human life. This conception of the human does not coincide with the biological understanding of human beings as a species (though of course the mode of our embodiment does matter tremendously to us). It also eludes the human as an easily available category of social science research. By contrast, the conception of the human we are concerned to isolate is essentially first personal (both singular and plural) in that it shows up in our living, imagining, and thinking, and in our emotional lives. It is essentially normative, too, in the sense that being human in this manner includes striving to live up to certain aspirations and ideals that characterize us as being *good* at being human, and being human in this sense as being good. The human in this sense is humane.

It is this sense of the human that the humanities try to bring to light—both as theoretical inquiry and as encouragement. It aims to clarify a certain mode of self-consciousness that we, as humans, share. This special sense of meaningfulness is one we learn, first of all, through being impressed by exemplars—by other people who seem to be shining forth in their own attempts to live a distinctively human life—and then through our own attempts in imagination, thought, conversation, and action to emulate and aspire to such lives ourselves. The humanities, when they are vibrant, form a family of communities that develop understandings of what it is to be human in this peculiar sense. Indeed, the activity of developing our understandings partially constitutes our humanity—so understood.

With all of this in mind, let us again consider the question: When did Meghan and Harry marry? To some, this question might seem silly or even unintelligible, and that too is an important fact. It shows that to such a person, the category of marriage has ceased to matter in the special sense of mattering we are trying to understand. It might continue to matter in other ways. For example, we can imagine a sociologist who believes that while marriage is an important social and historical institution—worthy of serious study—it is an institution that was formed in a religious context that has faded, and thus the question of *when* Meghan and Harry got married is no longer one that is particularly meaningful. Still, the sociologist might carry out rigorous empirical research about marriage, the social institution. Her research may have significant impact on, say, child health-care policy. But then what shows up as mattering to her in the special sense we are trying to track is her sense of *this sociological form of inquiry* being important to living a meaningful life (in this case, her own). Of course, these two senses in which marriage might be important—as something in which I might engage as part of my efforts to live a significant life and as a serious matter of theoretical inquiry—are not mutually exclusive in that they both may matter to a single person. But they are different manners of mattering.

It might seem clear that *at least as a social fact,* Meghan and Harry got married on the public occasion (the event of May 19, 2018). That is what has gone down in the official records. That is the date on the marriage certificate. It is what all the newspapers tell us, and we have it on no less an authority than the Archbishop of Canterbury, who says, "The legal wedding was on the Saturday. I signed the wedding certificate, which is a legal document, and I would have committed a serious criminal offence if I signed it knowing it was false."[2] One might think that that puts paid to any question of when the marriage as a social fact occurred. I am skeptical. Even in its public form, it is constitutive of marriage that to get married, both parties have to be in their right minds, understand that they are participating in a marriage, and take themselves to be agreeing to enter a marriage. (They may well be ambivalent or even think they are making a mistake, but they do think they are getting married.) But suppose two actors from the Royal Shakespeare Company were outside Lambeth Palace rehearsing a marriage scene that they planned to act on stage that evening. The Archbishop, walking by, misunderstood and—well-meaning fellow that he is—joined in. The actors mistook him for an actor who would be playing the priest. No matter what piece of paper the Archbishop signed as part of this misunderstanding, it would not turn the scene into a wedding. It would turn it into a farce.

Now, imagine the public occasion from Meghan and Harry's point of view. From their point of view, they could not possibly *get* married on their official wedding day because they already *were* married. They married three days previously, facilitated by the

Archbishop. A written document of those vows hangs on their wall. On the public occasion, they were only actors going through the motions, and the Archbishop was in on the act. The entire spectacle was a performance. But in that case, how could there possibly have been any kind of wedding—"legal" or not—if neither party thought they were getting married? The Archbishop gives casuistry a bad name. He says he cannot discuss confidential conversations he had with the couple. But the question is not about their private chatter; it is about whether he, three days before the public event, married them. In this context, his talk about the "legal" wedding sounds weaselly. So does his remark about committing a serious criminal offense if he knowingly signed a false document. How about all the intermediate cases, such as signing it without thinking all that much about it? *Archbishop!* I want to ask, in the eyes of God as best you understand it, when, if at all, did Meghan and Harry get married? Was the "legal" wedding the wedding, or did it occur three days before? In the Christian tradition, the answer to this question matters.[3]

In the *Nicomachean Ethics,* Aristotle tells us that in life we are all seeking happiness, though we may be unclear or confused about what it is. This striving shows up in what we do and how we live. Aristotle's conception of happiness (or *eudaimonia*) is complex, but it certainly includes achieving the kind of significance Meghan was striving for in her own efforts to have a real marriage. What kind of significance is that?

For Aristotle, happiness requires a self-conscious capacity to appreciate and participate in the *kalon.* This term is translated as "noble," "beautiful," or "fine" and, as I have suggested in Chapters 1–3, this variability reflects conceptual unease. Still, we can see Meghan striving for something correspondingly special (which we might call *kalon*) in her efforts to have a real marriage. The reality of the marriage, in her opinion, depended on it conforming to her idea of what makes marriage meaningful. In this context, I think we should consider the interview with Oprah not so much a retrospective report of an earlier event but a self-conscious elaboration of the event itself. Part of what it is to be *kalon* is to shine forth as such. In the very act of having this interview, Meghan manifests her belief that the whole world is capable of appreciating the specialness, the *rightness,* of her marrying as she chose to do. Of course, Aristotle thought that only a restricted elite would be able to appreciate the *kalon,* while Meghan insisted on a more egalitarian outlook. But the point about the importance of recognition remains. It is a way of building community.

Her act—that is, private ceremony plus public declaration on Oprah—was also intended as a critique. For thousands of years, a certain social sect in Europe has insisted that their conception of nobility (which nonaccidentally included themselves) was the truth about what nobility is. The official marriage between Meghan and Harry was meant to show how this form of nobility can adapt to the exigencies of modernity. In effect, Meghan insisted that there was something phony about this attempt at nobility. It had degenerated into spectacle. The real marriage—the true *nobility*—was the private event and its showing forth on Oprah.

At this point, we arrive at an important question about the availability of conceptual resources. In the case of Meghan, she clearly has the concepts of *marriage* and *authenticity* with which she wants to understand herself and have others understand her. It is with these in mind that she sought to break free of oppressive cultural norms and expectations. The issue is whether she gets trapped one level up: trying to escape a phony ritual on the basis of concepts that are themselves clichéd or distorted. She subverts the ritual only to be snagged by the concept. This is a problem that confronts us all.

In Plato's *Euthyphro*, Socrates encounters Euthyphro when the latter is on his way to court to sue his father for impiety. This act will have a potentially devastating impact on his family, and yet in conversation, it emerges that Euthyphro is living with a clichéd and confused conception of *piety*. At one level, Euthyphro is free to live according to his conception of what is pious, but one level up, he is a prisoner of his conception. Meghan with *authenticity* and *marriage* is in a similar position to Euthyphro just before he met Socrates. In Meghan's case, she earned celebrity, wealth, and personal prestige on her own; she was able, along with her husband, to structure a marriage as she saw fit. But what resources did she have to question what *marriage* and *authenticity* should mean? What freedom did she have with the concepts themselves? I ask this not just about her but because it is a problem that pervades our culture, and, more generally, it is a problem that haunts human social life. This brings us back to the importance and value of the humanities.

In her essay "Losing Your Concepts," the philosopher Cora Diamond has argued that one aspect of growing up in unjust conditions is that people often lack the concepts with which to understand their situations and themselves. Indeed, injustice is regularly sustained with concepts that distort and disfigure our understanding of what it is to live well. What reason do we have to trust (for example) our inherited idea of authenticity? And what to do if we take ourselves to be living in conditions of injustice? In modernity, the very concepts by which we organize our lives have become open to skeptical worry, and there seems to be no Archimedean point.

This may at first seem wildly counterintuitive, but I suggest as a way forward we return to the *kalon*. My reason for doing so will become clear by the end. It helps to distinguish three levels of the *kalon*. The distinction is for heuristic purposes only; in reality, there are interminglings and overlaps. At the first level, there are people striving in their lives for significance. They are trying to live happy lives in the deep, eudaimonistic sense of happy. Then, second, there are those whose first-level strivings take a peculiar turn: they survey the human scene and try to give it back to us in poetry and fiction, philosophy, art, and other narrative forms. Sometimes, they give us accounts of the *kalon* as exemplified in heroes and heroines, but that is not all. Sometimes, they portray humanity as a mixed bag of foibles, failings, and even evil, with perhaps a few moments of generosity and clarity. Nonetheless, there is something *kalon* about helping us understand ourselves better—whatever the truth brings. And then, third, there emerges this historical institution, the humanities, that is, of its own nature, dedicated to conserving (in some sense of "conserve") these special attempts to understand ourselves as human. It is a disciplined account of what we take to be our best first-personal attempts to understand the human.

What is it about this form of studying the human—both the *kalon* and its failures—that makes *it kalon*? I want to say that the humanities, properly understood, are a special form of mourning. And, perhaps surprisingly, mourning is a realm in which humans can achieve excellence. When we mourn well, it is a peculiarly human way of flourishing. I will stick with Aristotle not because I want to promote him above others but because with him I can speak from personal experience. Aristotle lived. While he lived, he tried to make sense of life. Then, he died. That would be it, completely it—as far as we can tell, in this world—but for the relentless activities to keep him alive in thought, imagination, and emulation by generations of scholars, teachers, and students, each passing on not only the teaching but the love of the learning from one generation to the next. In that sense, it is a matter of life and death. It is only because of all this activity that I am able to speak to you today about the *kalon* and why it might continue to matter to us.

In essence, mourning is one of the ways we exercise our capacity for love. We get attached to people and ideals, thoughts and projects that are themselves vulnerable. And we respond to that vulnerability by becoming active ourselves in making sense of what it all meant or will continue to mean. Other animals suffer loss; other animals grieve in complex ways. If we want, we can call that mourning. But our form of mourning is an attempt to turn loss into a reanimated gain—in imagination, thought, emotion and, importantly, symbolic expression. We make human meanings, and when we can share these meanings publicly, it is constitutive of the formation of culture. Aristotle lived; Aristotle died. It is only our activity that transforms this change into loss and into a certain kind of gain.

It is via these types of activities that we develop ourselves as historical beings. We are historical beings because we have pasts that matter to us—that is, pasts that partially constitute our present by shaping our sense of what is important. Thus mourning, when done well, is a special manner of our distinctive form of flourishing. It helps us come to clarity about what matters—in that special sense of mattering we are tracking. It is *kalon* to keep alive in thought and imagination the best attempts to understand the human from a first-personal human point of view. The humanities are a family of historical and cultural attempts to keep this form of mourning alive in a shared public arena. It is therefore a mistake to try to justify the humanities in instrumental terms by saying, for example, that if we study Aristotle, it will improve our critical thinking, and if we are better at critical thinking, we will do better in our careers. That may be true. But it misses what the humanities are about and what they ought to be about in our lives. As a form of mourning, the humanities enrich us with a lively sense of the finest attempts to understand what matters about living a human life, overcoming, while in another way maintaining, boundaries of space and time. But in all of it, *we ourselves* are engaged. It is essentially first-personal activity. In the case of the humanities (and to stick with the examples we have been using), it is not just that we get opened up to thousands of years of extraordinary thinking and artistic expression about what *marriage* and *authenticity* might mean in human life. When things are going well, we develop a capacity for critical playfulness, for re-creation and change of the very concepts with which we are thinking. We are freed up for a poetic reinterpretation of authenticity, as well as opened to the possibility of giving up the concept altogether and living according to different concepts. This is the manner of returning from preoccupation with loss (the past) to life (in the present). The point of the humanities, then, is not some goal external to it. The point of the humanities is that it itself is a mode of our flourishing.

So, to come back to Meghan, the issue is not that the humanities would have helped her *instrumentally* to make a more critically informed decision, as though she were solving a problem in Clue ("in the garden with the Archbishop" or "at the Palace, with the Queen"?). The question is not which is the right place (as though there were a correct answer existing independently of her deliberation), but rather what inner resources and cultural opportunities she was able to draw upon so as to turn the choice-making activity itself into a deep understanding of who she is, what her freedom and flourishing consists in, and, correlatively, what the world she lives in means.

To some, this may appear a trivial example centered on a shallow person. But I think such a perspective ignores something important. And this also bears on the question that frames our concern with the humanities: What is worth conserving? There are different ways one might understand this question, and some of them are, in my opinion, quite problematic. But to begin with a positive construal, one of the most important aspects of the humanities that needs conserving is the capacity to transmit a sense of its own importance, a sense of the joy and meaningfulness internal to it, from one generation to the next. The question of conservation here is not so much about *what* to teach but about *how*. Meghan is not unlike many students in our humanities courses. She is already struggling with issues about what would make her life meaningful, and she has not yet internalized the riches of the humanities. Whatever the conceptual resources or limitations of our students, these stirrings for significance should be seen not as grounds for skepticism but rather as an opportunity for us as teachers.

So, what is, above all, worth conserving in the humanities are teachers—*proper* teachers. In my experience, teachers do not emerge from classes on pedagogy (though they might be able to survive them). There are, I think, three overlapping features that make for an excellent teacher. The first is that they themselves are exemplars of the love of their subject. Many of the teachers who influenced me were not interested *in me* at all. But in their teaching, they put on display their fascination with and dedication to the area of study. There was something marvelous in their efforts to study and teach something they found marvelous. In a way, humanities professors ought to be first responders to students' hunger for the *kalon*—not just by giving them large-scale cultural exemplars but also by being exemplary in their manner of doing so. Linda Zagzebski has pointed out that with large-scale cultural exemplars, we can be struck by their beauty or nobility or special-ness before we understand what it is about them that is grabbing us. Here, I am less concerned with these alleged examples of supreme excellence, but rather want to focus instead on often very flawed characters we encounter in everyday life—our teachers—who, for all their foibles and sometimes bad behavior, do have a spark about them. Of course, that opens room for show-offs and se-ducers. But right now, I want to concentrate not on how things go wrong but how they go right when they do. Part of what it is for things to go right is for students to see right before their eyes a manifestation of something special shining forth, not that far off, as something they could imagine partaking in, perhaps in a dif-ferent form.

Second, as I said, the humanities are a manner of overcoming while maintaining boundaries of space and time. One of the impor-tant reasons for teaching the humanities in an undergraduate cur-riculum is that by and large, it is not the sort of thing one can pick up on one's own. One needs to be taught skills of reading and writing, thinking and imagining, so as to be able to enter distant worlds and—in some remarkable and unusual way—inhabit them from a distance as a mode of animating and deepening one's own life.

The third feature is really an elaboration of the second: one needs to teach students how to play. To return to Aristotle for a moment, it was important for me to learn how to read the Aristotelian texts, to struggle with getting it right, to immerse myself in ancient Greek conceptions of *psyche, eudaimonia,* and the *kalon,* and so on. But I was also encouraged into a certain kind of imaginary activity. What *might* Aristotle have thought about *this?* What if a new man-uscript were discovered? How might we *go on* in an Aristotelian spirit with a contemporary challenge? This imaginary activity is at once mournful and playful—the question of *who it is* we are keeping alive in our imaginations goes into an enlivening abeyance. (As Donald Winnicott taught us, we often do not need to answer the question, "Where, precisely, is Aristotle located?")

These three features of teaching provide a clue to the intrinsic value of learning the humanities. The point is not if you study the humanities, you will learn to think better and then it is more likely you will get promoted in your job, you will then become rich and famous, and *then* you can do what you want! Rather, it is that for human life to flourish, it requires more than instrumentality.

None of these considerations are conservative in the familiar political sense of advocating a fixed canon of "the greats." As I said above, there are ways of understanding the question "What is worth conserving?" that are problematic. I want to highlight one that—following Kierkegaard—I shall call an *aesthetic* reading. In this version, we in the humanities conceive of ourselves along the lines of curators at a great museum, or librarians at a great library, or professors at a great university. There are so many artworks already in our basement, but there is not enough wall space for the exhibition, or there are too many books for our shelves, or there is too much learning to fit into a curriculum, and we must make choices. But on the aesthetic reading, there are two unquestioned assumptions. First, it is left unquestioned what it means to conserve. We assume we already know what conserving is: the only issue is which items to choose. Second, it is assumed that the basis of choice will be educated judgment, but the question of what educated judgment consists in is left largely to the side. It is as though the question were about the worth of the various "objects" of the humanities as opposed to the worth of what we are doing in raising the question in this manner. It is that kind of questioning that is integral to the humanities, and it gets left out in what I have called the aesthetic reading.

By way of contrast, I have tried to provide an *ethical* reading of the question. What should count as *conserving* when we commit to the task of promoting human flourishing, both individually and living together in communities?[4] In this vein, let me conclude with a word about my continued use of the term *kalon*. My point is not nostalgic. I have no interest in "going back to ancient Greece," whatever that means. Rather, I want to use the term to signal a gap: an intuition that for reasons we may not comprehend, we may not have the concepts we need to understand our condition well. Each of the possible translations of *kalon* into English seems to me problematic. "Noble" carries connotations of thousands of years of European exploiters, thugs, and dissolutes giving meaning to the term by putting on furs and shiny rocks, making others bow down and call them "King" and "Queen." Good riddance to them! (And *go Meghan!*) "Beauty" carries with it the sense of an aesthetic beauty detached from the ethical. "Fine" signifies something good but is vague and thus does not pack the right aspirational punch. The point of my continuing to use the Greek word *kalon* is that it signals that we do have a hunch but that we do not yet know in sufficient detail *what it is* that we are looking for.

The aim here is not to recover Aristotle's conception in the hope of returning to it. The society Aristotle inhabited was also unjust. Therefore, one should suspect that his concept of the *kalon* was itself disfigured, with its connotation of "nobility" in particular legitimizing an unjust social hierarchy in which he partook. My own stance is Platonic is spirit. We should assume that both we and those from whom we might learn have been living in conditions of injustice that disfigure our attempts to understand what is good (in effect, we are all in the cave). Still, we can get glimpses of a good direction to follow. Using the *kalon* self-consciously as a signifier, not a fully developed concept, is a useful direction to proceed. We thereby signal to ourselves that we have a hunch that both they and we are onto something important about being human, but we are also in the midst of life and thus in the midst of confusions, contradictions, and unclarities. What seems to me worth conserving is the spirit of making our best efforts (according to our best reflective understandings of what we mean by "best") to travel all over the world—across space, time, and cultures—in study and imagination to discover and conserve what we take to be the deepest attempts of other humans to understand and express the human condition. It is a spirit of rigorous hope that, I believe, is itself a manifestation of our flourishing.

5

Good Mourning in Gettysburg and Hollywood

Introduction

When I was a boy, I learned the Gettysburg Address by heart. A teacher had assigned the task of memorizing it and speaking it out loud in front of the class. There are two aspects of that experience that I can articulate more clearly now. First, it felt good. There is a bodily dimension in declaiming another person's words, and when the prose is aspirational and has a nice cadence, one can feel pleasure in filling one's lungs and then pushing the words out into the social world. Second, I had only a dim understanding of what I was saying. "Four score and seven years ago" is a beautiful phrase, but I did not know what a score was. That did not matter much to me. Even now, when I say "four score and seven" it takes a moment to know what I am saying, in a way that saying "eighty-seven" does not. And there is still a kernel of pleasure when I recite that phrase in my mind.

This early memorization makes it such that I cannot go back to the Gettysburg Address without resonances of my childhood. This was a time just before the assassinations of John F. Kennedy, Martin Luther King, Robert Kennedy, and others, before anyone in the suburb had heard of a place called Vietnam. Whatever the injustices running through the country, it was a time and a neighborhood in which patriotism came easily. Many families had in recent generations escaped persecution in Europe, and they were eager to assimilate as Americans. We had no idea that the vindication we felt for being on the right side of the Civil War—and indeed in favor of the civil rights movement—facilitated blindness to racism in our midst. I am not a Civil War buff. So, that was it for me and Gettysburg until almost forty years later when I received a shock. Drew Faust gave me a copy of her book, *This Republic of Suffering*, and I read it.

The Dead Bodies of Gettysburg

The book is matter of fact in a historian's manner, and it examines the practical problem of dealing with the dead bodies of war. Faust describes the immediate aftermath of the Battle of Gettysburg: "By July 4, [1863] an estimated six million pounds of human and animal carcasses lay strewn across the field in the summer heat, and a town of 2,400 grappled with 22,000 wounded who remained alive but in desperate condition."[1] This was an extraordinary encounter of the living with the dead. There would have to be a series of burials and reburials. The first burial was carried out in haste and under an aura of necessity. The sun was hot, rain came in torrents, maggots and flies multiplied exponentially. The decomposition of approximately 7,000 soldiers' bodies was occurring at an alarming rate. In addition, there were 4,000 surviving soldiers who would soon die from wounds, as well as 3,000 dead horses strewn around the battlefield. The sense of necessity flowed from a threat to public health, as well perhaps from a more inchoate sense that these bodies had to be put underground right away.

In his book *A Strange and Blighted Land,* Gregory A. Coco assembled vivid first-personal accounts of the first attempts at burial. I shall give only a few examples:

. . . soldiers with their hands and feet sticking out of the ground, I do not say out of their graves for they had none, but were buried, if buried they were, where they lay by throwing a little dirt over their bodies; but the worst sight that I saw was a Con that had not been buried at all, most of his body was decayed, his head was disconnected from his body and on the whole presented the most horrid sight.[2]

Some of the men buried the dead thus laid in rows; a shallow grave about a foot deep, against the first man in a row and he was then laid down into it; a similar grave was dug where he had lain.[3]

[the dead] were so far decomposed that we had to run rails under their bodies, which, as they slid into the trenches broke apart, to the horror and disgust of the whole part, and the stench still lingers in our nostrils. As many as ninety bodies were thus disposed of in one trench . . . most of them were tumbled in just as they fell, with not a prayer eulogy or tear to distinguish them from so many animals.[4]

They dug long trenches about ten inches deep, they would lay from fifty to one hundred in each trench, then throw clay along the middle of the rows of men leaving the head and feet entirely exposed.[5]

Civic and political leaders knew there had to be a second burial—one that was proper, dignified, and symbolic. The details of the formation of Gettysburg National Cemetery are well documented.[6] The salient issue is that the Confederate dead were to be excluded from this reburial. This fact is easily knowable. But it came as a shock to me—in part, because that boy who used to be me, who filled his body with Lincoln's words, had no inkling that he was re-enacting a ritual that excluded the defeated, unburied, and poorly buried dead.

I admit to a certain horror at the image of these dead being left unburied or scantily buried—a sense that there is a wrong here too primordial to explain. The horror is in part with the *all rightness* of it all—with the fact that in that social world, people felt sufficiently comfortable living with this state of affairs (and opposed to doing anything more), even if they were living right there in Gettysburg. I suppose I could have heard a similar tale about people fighting in some faraway place in some ancient period, and it would not have made a such a difference to me. Part of the shock, then, was that of this having something to do with me, of this possibly being *my* past. My aim is not to judge these people. I have no views about whether they "could have done otherwise" and thus none about whether they "should have." And mourning does not require that such questions be answered.

The separation of the dead began in earnest at the end of October. An order had been issued in August forbidding the exhumation of bodies until the end of September. When the digging up of bodies did begin, the process of decomposition was already well advanced. Many of the soldiers could no longer be identified. Still, remnants of cloth or of a shoe, buttons, and the location of burial were used as the basis for separating the corpses that would be buried again from those that would not. Samuel Weaver who oversaw the exhumation attended to each corpse. At the end of his efforts, he wrote, "I firmly believe that there has not been a single mistake made in the removal of the soldiers to the Cemetery by taking the body of a rebel for a Union soldier."[7] He was talking about the removal and reinterment of 3,512 corpses. Even today, a guide at the National Cemetery will say that they think only nine mistakes were made. Whatever the ultimate accuracy of identifications, the point is that great care went into keeping Confederate bodies out. This meticulousness was internally connected to the sense of dignity of the project. William Saunders, the architect, aimed to design a cemetery of "simple grandeur," and the low markers radiating out in semicircles invite quiet respect. The semicircles were articulated into areas assigned to the states. There were almost a thousand soldiers who could not be identified by name or state, but insofar as a corpse could be identified by state, he was located within the state plot. There was no allotment for states in rebellion. The cemetery conveys a sense of serenity, but "serenity" was achieved by excluding thousands who were left to rot where they lay. So, the effort to provide a dignified reburial was in the very same act a refusal to allow there to be a public space in which to mourn the Confederate dead. This was not a secret to anyone. It was the way things were. Although there were in subsequent years a few remarkable voices of protest, overall, the anger, suffering, and resentment ran so deep that, as Faust says, "it seemed unimaginable that those who had tried to destroy the Union should be accorded the same respect as those who had saved it."[8] Yes, the *same* respect, but the ethical question is: Is there another form of respect that does not valorize?

At the time Lincoln arrived to give his dedicatory speech, the cemetery was not finished.

The aim had been to bury 100 bodies a day. And Thursday November 19 was only three and a half weeks after the reburials had commenced. Thus, many of the bodies that would eventually find their way to this cemetery were still out in the battlefields. The work of the diggers and undertakers would continue into the spring of 1864. So, Lincoln placed himself in the midst of an unfinished selective harvest: a division of the dead into those who were to be memorialized and those who were not. Lincoln's words facilitated the separation by aiming to vindicate it.

Being There

I made a trip to Gettysburg National Cemetery. The cemetery is a dignified semicircle on a hill that opens up a vista of rolling hills and fields, and a country town. If one stands in the midst of the cemetery and surveys the understated tombstones, one can contemplate the dead whose bodily remains lie below. There is an unmistakable *this-ness* to being there, standing on the very ground where these men fought, died, and were buried. The architect, William Saunders, had a definite idea where the cemetery should end, and today, fences mark boundaries. But are human intentions strong enough to set boundaries for the dead? As I spent days at Gettysburg, I did not just want to look down but to look up and out and over the fence. The ever-widening semicircle of the cemetery establishes a field of vision. It is a beautiful country scene. But in that autumn of 1863, that country had corpses scattered throughout. The cemetery was created with the intention of leaving many of them where they were, outside its grounds.

This was the context of the Gettysburg Address. Standing in the cemetery, my mind began to wander. I imagined a huge amphitheater of the dead extending out indefinitely into the countryside. The gorgeous semicircle of the official cemetery is the VIP section. It is meant to be a place of solemnity and dignity and honor. It is a place that encourages us—we, the living, who are standing there—to remember, to mourn, to let our minds wander. I began to wonder: What if the unburied dead laying out in the distance had been able to listen to Abraham Lincoln's speech? Would they have heard a different speech from the one I learned growing up, even though we were both exposed to the same words?

The Gettysburg Address of my childhood emphasizes the beginning and the end: "Four score and seven years ago, our fathers brought forth on this continent, a new nation, conceived in Liberty, and dedicated to the proposition that all men are created equal. Now we are engaged in a great civil war, testing whether that nation or any nation so conceived and so dedicated, can long endure . . . that this nation, under God, shall have a new birth of freedom—and that government of the people, by the people, for the people, shall not perish from the earth." Lincoln was *imagining the end*—the end of political life—in both senses of "end." The first sentence emphasizes that the United States was constituted as a nation for the sake of a self-conscious purpose or end: to instantiate the ideals of freedom and equality in political life. But what is at stake in all this carnage is whether this nation or any nation so conceived and so dedicated can long endure. That is, must any nation organized around democratic ends necessarily come to an end due to its own internal divisions and strife? Can a government of the people, by the people, and for the people avoid perishing from the Earth?[9]

But now, as I tried to imagine an unburied soldier listening, he ceased to be an indefinite figure and began to take on a particular form. I could see him under a tree out in the distance, and I somehow knew his first name was Polynices and he came from Thebes, a small town in the South. For him, the emphasis of Lincoln's Address fell not on any one sentence or other, but rather on Lincoln's use of the plural pronoun and definite article:

. . . for *those* who here gave their lives . . .

. . . *the* brave men, living or dead who struggled here, have
consecrated it . . .

. . . but it [the world] can never forget what *they* did
here . . .

It is for us the living, rather, to be dedicated here to the
unfinished work which *they* who fought here have thus
far so nobly advanced.

. . . that from *these* honored dead we take increased
devotion . . .

. . . that we highly resolve that *these* dead shall not have
died in vain.

How, Polynices wanted to know, could Lincoln keep using the
words "they," "these," "those," and "the" and leave him out? *There
he was!* And yet, "these" and "those" did not seem to apply to him.
How could this be?

Polynices's question, as I understand it, is not about Lincoln the
man—his choices, psychology, motives, or character. Nor is it a
question about what anyone could have or should have done. His
question is semantic—about the relation of language and world.
How could it be that in this ghastly field of death and suffering,
any use of "these dead" or "those who died here" or "they who
fought here" could single out one group and exclude another?
How could language, with its words "these dead," not acknowledge *these* dead?

It might seem that the answer to this question is easy. "These
dead" is short for "these Union dead" and from the context of Lincoln's speech, one can tell that it is they whom Lincoln is talking
about. "These dead" are those who are to be buried in this cemetery. The scene may be dreadful, but there is no problem in picking

out the right group with the phrase "these dead." But, for Polynices, this answer misses his question. He understands these semantic
rules and practices. His horrified puzzlement might be expressed
thus: In the face of this destruction, how could the normal semantic rules continue to hold?

This is what the philosopher Cora Diamond has called the
difficulty of reality.[10] Polynices's "difficulty" is in grasping how, in
the face of the destruction that befell him and the other soldiers,
the concept of *death* could possibly comprehend, encompass,
give the living that with which *to think death*—and yet to think it
in such a way so as to be able to include some and exclude others.
It is as though reality overwhelms the concepts that are trying to
comprehend it.

A Problem Internal to the Gettysburg Address

In his words Lincoln tried to contain death and give it meaning.
He says, "The world will little note, nor long remember what we
say here, but it can never forget what *they* did here." This line rings
with sincerity and humility, but it cannot be true. Insofar as the
world will never forget, it will be via an interpretation of what happened and why it mattered. The Gettysburg Address puts itself
forward as the interpretation of what we should never forget. It is
clear that Lincoln intended the "they whom we can never forget"
to refer to the Union dead. Internal to the Gettysburg Address is
a refusal to acknowledge the excluded Confederate dead. And yet,
I want to argue, the Gettysburg Address cannot leave them out and
succeed at its own task. The point here is not to criticize Lincoln
or to say what he should have done instead. Rather, it is to make
an ethical point about how *we* should continue to live with the
Gettysburg Address. The issue is how to inherit it now.

It is clear from his words that Lincoln took the very possibility of democratic political life to be at stake. It would be a devastating reckoning if any society organized around the ideals of equality and liberty was thereby threatened with extinction. For this "new nation" that "our fathers brought forth" was not merely an addition to the list of nations on Earth but a new type of nation. Instead of being organized for the sake of a few around a fraudulent claim of entitlement, this "new nation" aimed at ends that were at once fine, noble, beautiful, *and available to all citizens.* Throughout this book, I have been using the signifier *kalon* in Socratic acknowledgment that in an important sense, we do not yet know what we are talking about. We are living with a concept in the midst of its own historical development, a concept with aspirations that we recognize have not yet been adequately worked out. We participate in these aspirations, in part, by acknowledging they are not fully within our grasp either.

Lincoln's "new nation" democratized the possibility of living a noble life. The ends open to every citizen to pursue—liberty and equality—are themselves *kalon.* And since what it would be to pursue these ends *well* would be precisely to pursue them freely and with due regard to the equality of others, the possibility of living a life that was itself *kalon* ought to be widely available among the citizenry. To put it in modern parlance, we all share the entitlement to (and should share the possibility of) living a *meaningful* and *worthwhile* life—one recognized and honored by others. This is one reason why it is so important that a government of the people, by the people, and for the people should not perish from the Earth.

But if the possibility of a *kalon* life becomes more democratically available, so too do the possibilities of failed attempts, misses, and misfires. Generally speaking, the *kalon* is not a source of anxiety when it is assumed to be way out of reach. But if the *kalon* both becomes more democratically available yet, in its own ways, remains difficult to achieve, the culture has had little practice in knowing how to accommodate and publicly acknowledge the many ways we can fail. If we consider the poorly buried Confederate dead strewn over the fields of Gettysburg, it seems fair to say that none of them lived a *kalon* life, although they were likely striving for it. Part of what it is to lead a *kalon* life is to live a life organized toward a cause that is itself *kalon*. Whatever else one might say about the causes for which they fought, it contained a profound evil, slavery, and no life organized so as to promote it could possibly be *kalon*. They pursued an end they mistakenly thought was honorable. They sacrificed their lives mistakenly thinking a terrible evil was a good. The *kalon* has no room for such terrible error.

In writing about this, I have been accused of having sympathy for the Confederate cause or for being insensitive to the evil of slavery.[11] This is not true. I do, however, have sympathy for people who are trying to live a *kalon* life but who, for historical and cultural reasons, along with character flaws of their own, get caught in a vision that is wildly wrong and profoundly unjust due to misunderstandings and misperceptions and social pressures—and then waste their lives, sometimes doing terrible harm, in a cloud of misapprehension and falsity.

We live in times in which the possibility of such failure touches us all. The call of the unburied Confederate dead is, in part, simply the call of the unburied dead. In part, it is also, as I shall argue, the call of *our* unburied dead (what it is to be a nation, albeit polarized). But it is also the call of the difficult case: the call to recognize that *even here,* where a person's end was bad and he inflicted terrible harm on others, he was also making a terrible mistake. He may be responsible for his error, but he was not doing evil for the sake of doing evil; he did evil under misapprehension he was doing something good, even *kalon*. To leave such people unburied is to acknowledge that we have not yet figured out how to mourn them. Certainly, no hint of valorization should attach to them. (So, nothing in this position opposes removing from public squares all monuments that valorize the Confederate cause and those who fought for it.) But if we do not have some form of public memory for those who tried yet horribly failed to achieve an enigmatic good, how are we to learn from their failures? The possibility of doing great harm while thinking one is doing good is a real and pervasive human possibility. It marks us as human. What are we to do with it?

The point, then, is not to judge those who refused to bury the Confederate dead. Rather, it is an attempt to mourn the mourners—as well as mourn those whom they mourned and those whom they refused to mourn. It is an attempt to figure out a way to be with the dead who themselves were trying to figure out how to be with the dead. About this too, one can be confused. I suspect that the refusal to mourn flowed not simply from the understandable fury of the northerners, but also from a culturally constricted sense of what providing a proper burial would mean. Our modes of memorializing the dead tend in the direction of celebrating them—of glorifying, honoring, and idealizing them. Thus far, we seem to lack modes of public acknowledgement that these dead matter, and we must take them into account, even if we do not want in any way to vindicate them.

Lincoln wrote two copies of the Gettysburg Address before he delivered it out loud.[12] There is a comma in the first draft—the Nicolay copy—that gets omitted in subsequent drafts: "We come to dedicate a portion of it, as a final resting place for those who

died here, that the nation might live." Whatever Lincoln's intentions, that second comma in this first draft holds open the thought
that we need a final resting place for those who died here—that is,
for *all who died here*—in order for our nation to live. This is the
beginning of a profound thought: that strange and counterintuitive and even offensive as it first might seem, we need to provide a
final resting place, even for those who fought against us (in part,
because they nevertheless are us)—in spite of the fact and acknowledging the fact that they killed our loved ones and our heroes, in
spite of the terrible fact that they supported a terrible cause. And
we need to do this not only out of elemental human decency, but
also in order that the nation might live. On this reading, the vi-
tality of the nation depends on our finding adequate ways to offer
a final resting place for the Confederate dead.

The possibility of this reading is eliminated in the second draft,
the Hay copy: "We have come to dedicate a portion of it, as a final
resting place for those who here gave their lives that that nation
might live." The aim is now specified as dedicating a final resting
place for those who here *gave their lives that that nation might live*.
That is certainly not what the Confederates had been doing. So,
this sentence becomes a statement of the principle of division and
separation.

And yet, there is a countervailing thought that persists throughout
the Address. Lincoln famously says that it is *our fathers* who
brought forth this new nation. So, he describes the nation as a
family affair. But then, who gets to count as the descendants? It is
internal to the idea of family that the descendants remain family,
even if they begin to fight among each other. One might try to
object that the only true descendants are those who endorse the
proposition that all men are created equal. This strains at the idea
of family, but in any case, it is not the route Lincoln went down.

He insists on conceiving of this strife as "a great civil war"—that is, as a fight among ourselves. And he certainly intended that when the war was won, when peace was restored and the rebellious states were again an uncontested part of the United States, that the citizens there would count as descendants of "our fathers" who brought forth this nation. What, then, to think of their immediate fathers, the ones who were left dead and unburied on the battlefield?

Lincoln's conceptualization transforms this scene of carnage into a mythic, tragic structure. The unburied Confederate corpse over there is a family member, and thus there hangs over this scene the specter of a primordial wrong, refusing to bury a family member. This is the stuff of Sophoclean tragedy. And it haunts Lincoln's use of the phrase "a final resting place for those who died here" to mean these *and not those.*

The political consequences of this exclusion are well known. After the war, women's memorial associations sprung up throughout the South—in effect, a Southern sisterhood of Antigones. Though their official mission was to rebury and honor the Confederate dead, they became, as Faust recounts, "a means of keeping sectionalist identity not just alive, but strong."[13] "Ensuring the immortality of the fallen and of their memory," she continues, "became a means of perpetuating southern resistance to northern domination and to the reconstruction of southern society."[14] In the case of Gettysburg, the Hollywood Memorial Association of the Ladies of Richmond (Virginia) made it their business to secure proper reburials for the Confederate dead.[15] The reinterments occurred eight to ten years after the battle, in the period 1871–1873. There was widespread anxiety about the fate of the corpses. The Gettysburg side of the reinterments was directed by Dr. Rufus Weaver, the son of Samuel Weaver who oversaw the original reburials of the Union dead at Gettysburg. Dr. Weaver sent the remains of 2,273 Confederate bodies to Hollywood Cemetery, and altogether, he exhumed 2,935 Confederate bodies for reburial. He was never fully paid for his efforts.[16] Hollywood Cemetery provided a point of focus for glorifying the nobility and ideals of the so-called lost cause, which included of course deep resentment against the North. So, "the problem" of the unburied and poorly buried Confederate dead was "resolved" via a massive effort and a geographical separation.

I made a trip to Hollywood Cemetery—to the "Gettysburg Hill" that is to be found in the midst of a Virginia graveyard. In some ways, it is a mirror image of Gettysburg. The tombstones are discrete, though in Hollywood, there are inscriptions of CSA and of southern states, ARK or Texas or VA or MISS. In Hollywood, small Confederate flags on sticks are planted all around. But, truly, the discrete honorings of the Confederate dead were uncannily like the discrete honorings of the Northern dead at Gettysburg. The irony was that geographical separation was necessary for the sake of preserving the same mode of mourning in both places. In this way, the two cemeteries were united. They were, and still are, stuck in a rigid insistence that mourning can only occur as valorization. This was the key to many otherwise strange phenomena: how it could be that "Gettysburg Hill" is in Richmond, Virginia; how particles of Gettysburg soil found their way to be part of Gettysburg Hill; why the corpses needed to come all this way to be mourned; how there could be row after row of gravestones of men who died up close, fighting each other—with the same dates, July 1 and July 3, 1863, so often inscribed—that were separated by 180 miles. The Confederates had found a way back "home": a place determined to valorize their memory.[17] One sees small rocks, sometimes flowers, placed on top of markers and tombs all around to let visitors know that they are still being used as sites of mourning.

There was one memorial plaque in Hollywood that was an exception to this funerary logic of division and separation. It had been laid down only recently, in 2015. I quote it in full:

Dr. Rufus Benjamin Weaver, 1841–1936

At the end of the War Between the States, plans were made to return the Confederate dead from Gettysburg. Ladies Memorial Associations and many veterans began to raise funds and to petition the federal government to let the remains be brought home.

Samuel Weaver, who retrieved the Union dead, was their choice to supervise the task. Before he could start, he was killed in a railroad accident. The grisly work then fell to his son, Dr. Rufus B. Weaver. He was to be paid $3.25 for each body shipped south.

As a Doctor of Anatomy, he proved to be the right man. At the opening of each grave, he ensured all remains possible were located. Overcoming many obstacles, he exhumed and sent South, the remains of 3,320 Soldiers. 2935 came to Richmond.

As the bodies were returned, Major General George E. Pickett met each shipment, and led a procession of old Veterans, Dignitaries, and Richmond Citizens, following the dead to Hollywood Cemetery. Pickett lies with these men today on "Gettysburg Hill"—

Dr. Weaver was paid for the first year, but then due to a Depression that hit the nation, funding ceased. Ultimately he received about one half of what he was owed. From his own resources, he continued his noble work.

In grateful appreciation, acknowledging a debt of honor owed by all Southerners and recognizing his generosity and humanity, the Sons of Confederate Veterans, place this marker in honor of Dr. Rufus B. Weaver.

—2015—

It is a gruesome irony that General Pickett who sent so many of these men to their deaths was there to welcome them home. But, as to Dr. Weaver, the plaque says that even after funding ceased, he "continued his *noble* work." Like every gravestone in both cemeteries, this too is an attempt to recognize and honor the *kalon* as manifest in the acts of an individual human being. But the *kalon* for which Dr. Weaver is memorialized is not for fighting on either side of the Civil War, but rather for respecting the dignity of a dead soldier, no matter what side he fought for. He is honored for respecting the humanity of a human being (even in the case of burying a former enemy).[18] This was a recognition that could cross an otherwise polarized divide: "Sons of Confederate Veterans" honoring a Northern doctor. The Weaver plaque is primarily an expression of gratitude: for Weaver's respectful work with the remains of the dead, for his continued dedication after funds had dried up, and, perhaps above all, for his "generosity and humanity." This was his "noble work." This was the one marker I saw that could be at either cemetery.

Dedication

It was Lincoln's aim in the Gettysburg Address to transform the audience's understanding of what the ceremony was about. The audience arrived thinking they were at the dedication of a cemetery. Lincoln demurred: "But, in a larger sense, we cannot dedicate—we cannot consecrate—we cannot hallow—this ground. The brave men, living and dead, who struggled here, have consecrated it, far above our poor power to add or detract." Instead, Lincoln urged, we should understand this as occasion *for us* to dedicate ourselves. "It is for us the living, rather, to be dedicated here to the unfinished work which *they who fought here* have thus far *so nobly* advanced. It is rather for us to be here dedicated to the great task remaining before us—that *from these honored dead* we take increased devotion to that cause for which they gave the last full measure of devotion—that we here highly resolve that *these dead* shall not have died in vain—."

As I understand Lincoln's Address, the intended transformation was not just in the meaning of the ceremony in terms of its content—"what it is about"—but in its practical meaning: encouraging a renewed commitment to act. The enduring question is how to succeed at that task.

On one of my visits to Gettysburg Cemetery, I took an early-evening tour with a park ranger. His talk was full of historical facts until we came to the end. At that point, the ranger took off his hat, extended both arms straight in front of him, and lustily declaimed the Gettysburg Address. He spoke the same words I did as a boy. When he got to "shall not perish from the earth," the audience applauded enthusiastically. What had just happened? I could not tell for sure. But it seemed to me that what occurred was a dramatization that elicited pleasurable feelings in speaker and audience alike, but which *substituted* for dedication, without anyone recognizing anything was missing. The recitation was getting in the way of the address of the Gettysburg Address. For the Gettysburg Address to succeed, the audience would need to feel itself targeted: called to "the great task remaining before us," promoting freedom and equality. The motivating power of such a call would be a sense of the *kalon.*

New Birth . . .

Lincoln enjoins us to "highly resolve . . . that this nation, under God, shall have a new birth of freedom." Part of what it would be to dedicate ourselves would be to figure out what this phrase means. It is clear that by "this nation," Lincoln meant all the states, including those currently in rebellion, reunited as a nation. But then, our dedication ought to be not only to promoting the ideals of freedom and equality, but also to promoting them in a nation that has become sufficiently reunited so as to constitute *this nation.* In short, some kind of reconciliation is a necessary precondition for the pursuit of freedom and equality.

Lincoln calls for a *new* birth, not a rebirth. This is not to be a flawed repetition of the original birth, which was itself disfigured by its toleration of slavery. But how do we avoid another flawed act if we exclude from recognition those whose ancestors and descendants are to be part of *this* nation? It would seem that maintaining fidelity to the spirit of Lincoln's call requires that we attend to *those* dead whom Lincoln's words tried to exclude. We do this *not* because we have sympathy for their cause but in recognition that to promote freedom and equality *in this nation* is to facilitate a shared historical understanding of what our struggles with freedom and equality have been. If we restrict ourselves to glorifying narratives of remembrance, we promote polarization: seeing those on the other side as a "basket of deplorables." We thereby stultify our own historical development as a nation committed to equality and liberty. We need thus to find a way to delink mourning and valorization. This means learning how to mourn in a public context failed attempts at the *kalon*. Only then can we find an appropriate mode to mourn the absence of mourning.

Even at the time, there were remarkable voices of conscience coming from the North about the treatment of the bodies of the Confederate dead.[19] Ironically, the most eloquent plea came from General George Meade who led the Union forces at Gettysburg. Speaking in July 1869, six years after the battle, four years after the war, and shortly before the reinterments to Hollywood began, Meade said of the Confederate dead:

> Why should we not collect them [Confederate bodies] in some suitable place? I do not ask that a monument be erected over them. I do not ask that in any way we should endorse their cause or their conduct or entertain other than feelings of condemnation for their cause. But they are dead; they have gone before their Maker to be judged. In all civilized countries it is usual to bury the dead with decency and respect, and even to fallen enemies respectful burial is accorded in death. I earnestly hope that this suggestion may have some influence throughout this broad land, for this is only one among a hundred crowded battlefields. Some person may be designated by the government, if necessary, to collect these neglected bones and bury them without commemorative monuments, but simply indicate that below sleep the misguided men who fell in battle for a cause over which we triumphed.[20]

There are several layers to Meade's thought. First, we should bury them simply because they were human, and they are now dead.[21]

This is the call of human to human, across battle lines, to recognize the significance of death. Second, we should regard them as *misguided men.* We bury them with "decency and respect" because they are human, but part of what it is to be human is to be capable of committing oneself to false images of the good. This capacity of mistaking bad for good is one we all share—and we can recognize that fact about our shared condition and still condemn the cause for which they fought. We can leave ultimate judgments about the value of their lives to some other realm (their "Maker"). Third, there is a need for some form of public recognition—not commemoration or valorization, but as a way to "simply indicate" that here lie men who fought for a cause that, fortunately, was defeated.

Our challenge is to create forms of memorializing that do not thereby valorize. It is part of dedicating ourselves to promoting equality and freedom in a nation that again, and perhaps forever, needs reuniting. It is an irony of our condition as historical and ethical beings that precisely in our dedication to overcome racist inequality we need (among many other things!) to find appropriate ways to mourn the absence of mourning of the Confederate dead. Mourning the absence of mourning thus becomes part of our "unfinished task."

Creative people will figure out better answers, but to get started, I suggest a plaque at the edge of Gettysburg Cemetery that looks out onto the battlefields that says something like this:

At the time of the founding of this cemetery and for
decades after only the bodies of those men thought to be
Union Soldiers were buried here and at National
Cemeteries throughout the country.

There were voices at the time that suggested respectful burials for the Confederate dead. Here are the words of General George Meade who led the Union forces at Gettysburg speaking in 1869.
[Quote from General Meade]
The country did not follow that advice at the time, but we now hereby recognize those Confederate soldiers whom Meade asked us to think of as "misguided men."

On an adjoining plaque a short quote from Lincoln:

. . . let me say I think I have no prejudice against the Southern people. They are just what we would be in their situation. If slavery did not now exist amongst them, they would not introduce it. If it did now exist amongst us, we should not instantly give it up. This I believe of the masses north and south. Doubtless there are individuals, on both sides, who would not hold slaves under any circumstances; and others who would gladly introduce slavery anew, if it were out of existence. We know that some southern men do free their slaves, go north, and become tip-top abolitionists; while some northern ones go south, and become most cruel slave-masters.

—Abraham Lincoln, Speech on the Kansas–Nebraska Act (October 1854)

What speaks in favor of learning how to mourn failed attempts at the *kalon* is that it brings us into imaginative contact with those who were striving for meaningful lives yet failed. Since we are vulnerable to just such a life, it would be good for us to understand better how this happens. We need room for a more nuanced understandings of how these failures could happen without in any way glorifying the person or false images of the good. Mourning, properly understood, is for the sake of *bidding adieu* and returning to life. It is the opposite of the glorification of a "lost cause" that keeps one stuck in melancholic fixation on an ideal that should be rejected.

I think back to myself as a boy memorizing the Gettysburg Address, and I wonder how differently I would have been formed if I *also* had to memorize and declaim that passage from Lincoln's speech on the Kansas–Nebraska Act.

. . . of *Freedom*

I conclude with a thought about what it is to dedicate ourselves to a new birth of *freedom*. Gary Wills argued that in the Gettysburg Address, Lincoln took us back to the founding ideals of the Declaration of Independence: liberty and equality. But it is an outstanding ethical challenge to determine what it should mean for us to "return" to those ideals and thereby dedicate ourselves to "the great task remaining before us." The original founders' dedication to these ideals was not, in their eyes, incompatible with being slaveholders, and we do not want to return to that. Equally obviously, we do know the general direction of immediate next steps in our dedication—promoting equality in access to education, to health care, and to basic economic opportunities—even if we might not yet know the best ways to achieve them. There is plenty we can do right now and throughout our lives in dedicating ourselves to these ideals. Still, it is internal to the concepts *freedom* and *equality* that there is an open-endedness that stretches out beyond the horizons of our imagination. If things go well, we should hope future generations will understand freedom and equality better than we do precisely because they are living in ways that so much better instantiate them. So, in dedicating ourselves now to this "unfinished work," we need to acknowledge that part of what is unfinished are the very ideals to which we are dedicating ourselves. This imposes a constraint on the structure of our hopes. In so dedicating ourselves, we can sincerely say that we hope for the unfolding of freedom and equality, but we need to recognize that we do not and cannot yet know all that well what we are hoping for.

6

The Difficulty of Reality and a Revolt against Mourning

It is internal to life that we face difficulties, obstacles, frustrations and, sometimes, adversity. For Aristotle, these need not get in the way of happiness. Indeed, they may set out the field in which happy lives are lived. Practically speaking, what it is for us to live in the world is to recognize ourselves in an environment over which we have at best very partial control, an environment that poses threats, offers opportunities, and challenges us with accidents and inevitabilities. The virtuous person will be excellent in meeting life's challenges. This is what living well consists in. Dealing with life's issues, then, is not preliminary to living a happy life; it is a happy life—at least, for some range of problems and some ways managing them.

Aristotle does not, of course, treat all difficulties as though they were there for our edification. He also thinks the world can be the source of great misfortunes, indeed catastrophes, that will destroy the happiness of even the most resilient among us. The consolations Aristotle offers are, first, that the virtuous will be best able to take in stride those difficulties thrown their way and, second, that when the virtuous are struck down by catastrophe and their happiness destroyed, they will maintain a certain dignity[1] (see Chapter 3).

Aristotle thought that our happiness is also vulnerable to misfortunes that befall our friends, loved ones, and descendants, and there might be nothing we can do (or could have done) to prevent it. He entertains the thought that such misfortunes might affect us even when we are dead, though he suspects they would not be such as to turn a man who died happy into a dead unhappy person.[2]

In the *Poetics,* Aristotle shows us how certain classic disasters can be turned into great art by rendering the plot intelligible. It is this form of intelligibility that makes possible a catharsis through pity and fear. But it does not follow that he believes that all terrible misfortune can be so redeemed. There are terrible misfortunes that can just befall one, by accident. They destroy one in an instant—along with all prospects for the happiness of oneself and one's loved ones. And yet there is not much more to say than "It was an earthquake." These are real dangers in Aristotle's world. He does not focus on them in the *Ethics* because for practical purposes they are not the sort of circumstances from which we can learn much, and he does not focus on them in the *Poetics* because they are not the circumstances from which one can create great tragedy.

It is important to understand that Aristotle's spectrum of suffering is not truncated. That insight will help us grasp a different kind of threat to the prospects for human happiness—that which the philosopher Cora Diamond has called "the difficulty of reality."[3]

Diamond is not expanding the bandwidth of Aristotle's spectrum; she is drawing our attention to a different dimension of experience. She is concerned with "the experience of the mind's not being able to encompass something which it encounters." She calls *the difficulty of reality* "experiences in which we take something in reality to be resistant to our thinking or possibly even painful in its inexplicability, difficult in that way, or perhaps awesome and astonishing in its inexplicability." She also speaks of its "being hard or impossible or agonizing to get one's mind around." Her emphasis is less on the psychological state of the sufferer than on *the difficulty of reality* to which that suffering bears witness.[4] Her concern is with the fit between the mind and the reality it seeks to comprehend.

Diamond begins her essay "The Difficulty of Reality and the Difficulty of Philosophy" by considering a poem by Ted Hughes, "Six Young Men." Allow me to quote from the beginning of her essay[5]:

The speaker in the poem looks at a photo of six smiling young men, seated in a familiar spot. He knows the bank covered with bilberries, the tree and the old wall in the photo; the six men in the picture would have heard the valley below them sounding with rushing water, just as it still does. Four decades have faded the photo; it comes from 1914. The men are profoundly, fully alive, one bashfully lowering his eyes, one chewing a piece of grass, one "is ridiculous with cocky pride" (1.6). Within six months of the picture's having been taken, all six were dead. In the photograph, then, there is thinkable, there is seeable, the death of the men. See it, and see the worst "flash and rending" (1.35) of war falling onto these smiles now forty years rotted and gone.

Here is the last stanza:

> That man's not more alive whom you confront
> And shake by the hand, see hale, hear speak loud,
> Than any of these six celluloid smiles are,
> Nor prehistoric or fabulous beast more dead;
> No thought so vivid as their smoking blood:
> To regard this photograph might well dement,
> Such contradictory permanent horrors here
> Smile from the single exposure and shoulder out
> One's own body from its instant and heat.

There is no place on Aristotle's spectrum of happiness (and unhappiness) to locate the poet's suffering. The problem is not that the spectrum is too narrow. There is no answer to the question whether the poet is suffering more or less than Priam. It is rather that the structure of happiness and unhappiness, of living in the world, is upended. I imagine a situation that began straightforwardly enough and then got out of hand. The poet began by looking back through an aging photograph to an earlier moment. It is a picture of an idyllic *before* when the young men were gay, jostling about, and had no idea what was about to befall them. The poet is in the position of knowing what they could not have known, trying to establish his own relation to the past, thinking about what happens to people. Perhaps he was mourning. Overall, he was in the midst of orienting himself—in time, in space, and in his emotional life. Somehow, the expected process goes awry. There is disorientation. The concepts *past* and *present, alive* and *dead, here* and *not here* cease to perform the discriminatory tasks they are normally deployed to perform.

What we have here is an eruption of the issue-laden nature of our being.[6] What is it for us to have a past? What is it for us to be dead? These are not just puzzles that we may never solve. They arrive in the manner of anxious confrontation. What the poet is experiencing is the breakdown of our normal use of concepts to contain the issues that are fundamentally our issues. The experience of the poem is extraordinary, but it is crucial not to lose focus on what the poetized experience is an experience of: the mind's inadequacy to encompass reality. This is what makes it a difficulty *of reality* and not simply one person's difficult experience in relationship to reality. That is why it is a mistake to focus exclusively on the psychological state of the person having this experience. When the poet picks up the photograph, he works his way to incoherence. The fabric of things starts to unravel. The poet insists there are "contradictory permanent horrors here"—and each word deserves emphasis. The horrors are *here,* confronting one; they are contradictory and they shall never be resolved.

> That man's not more alive whom you confront
> And shake by the hand, see hale, hear speak loud,
> Than any of these six celluloid smiles are,
> Nor prehistoric or fabulous beast more dead;

This is what Cora Diamond means by trying "to bring together in thought what cannot be thought." It is not an abstract effort to think "P" and "not P." Nor is "cannot be thought" a specifically psychological limitation. Rather, it is a self-conscious mode of unhappiness that recognizes of itself that it cannot be located within the standard structure of happiness and unhappiness.

Diamond makes it clear that it is possible to encounter the photograph so that one is not disturbed in the peculiar manner she is trying to isolate. "It is a photo of men who died young, not long after the picture was taken. Where is the contradiction?"[7]

I can imagine someone saying that it may be difficult *emotionally speaking* but it is not difficult *to understand*. In effect, such a person insists the concepts of *life* and *death* hold firm as we normally use them. There are four lessons to take away from this example. First, it may be rare for a person to experience the difficulty of reality (as Diamond understands it), and even rarer for the person to find a way to express it. Second, there are available means within the context of life to keep such experiences at a distance. Third, if we are turned away from the difficulty of reality, it will be tempting to interpret someone who is experiencing such difficulty—in this instance, the poet—in psychological terms, in terms of his individual suffering. For if we do not experience this person's difficulty as being *with reality*, then the interpretive pressure is overwhelming to see the suffering as idiosyncratic to this person. Finally, this difficulty erupts in the midst of the everyday. It is not like King Priam's situation, which we easily recognize as dramatically extraordinary and at the outer bounds of human grief. The occasion of the poem, by contrast, arises from looking at a photograph, taken of people forty years earlier—people whom the poet has long known to have been long dead. This is what we do with photographs; it is part of life as we know it. Somehow, our ordinary dealings with death erupt and, most important, make manifest in their disruption the mind's inadequacy to its task.

It should be clear by now that Diamond uses the phrase *difficulty of reality* in an unusual sense. Normally, when we think of difficulties, we think of aspects of the world that are either difficult to deal with or difficult to understand. We think of problems to be solved or resolved. Theoretically speaking, consider the difficulties—*aporiai*—with which Aristotle begins a scientific treatise: these are aspects of the world that are not yet transparent to us. What it is to be a world is to contain difficulties in this sense;

difficulties that get resolved as the world becomes more intelligible to us. Practically speaking, difficulties may be threatening, horrifying, or overwhelming, but they do not normally present reality as too much for our concepts. Diamond is trying to awaken us to an experience of inadequacy in human conceptual life itself.

So, there is the difficulty of reality, and then there is the difficulty of reality. The first is a normal problem in the world; the second is an anxious disruption of those normal forms. For this latter sense, the poet (Ted Hughes) and the philosopher (Cora Diamond) talk of being *shouldered out.* But these two senses of *the difficulty of reality* are related. The latter experience can grow out of the former in a breakdown. "How *could* they have died?! How could *they* have died!?"

It is only after a while that the poet is shouldered out. Conversely, the latter experience of difficulty can evanesce back into the former as one flees, or perhaps simply tires, of the strong experience of difficulty. Somehow, one finds oneself back in the normal order of things, ruminating about a picture of six young men.

It is also true that *the difficulty of reality* in the strong sense of that phrase itself has layers of meaning, Reality is *there,* difficult, a challenge to the mind's ability to comprehend. But reality is also *actively being* difficult.

> Such contradictory permanent horrors here
> Smile from the single exposure and shoulder out
> One's own body from its instant and heat.

This is not merely an account of a person being driven crazy; it is mind's report of casualty from a battlefront of understanding. The wounding is internal to reality. It is not simply the failure of a transcendent mind to grasp a difficult independent object.

Such a gaze can *shoulder out:* what does this mean? How could this expression acquire this use? I am not here inquiring about the poet's genius but rather about how the word has been used so as to make it possible for the poet to deploy it as he does. Shoulder. Soldier. Soldiers shoulder soldiers out. They have been practicing all their lives; in locker rooms, on playing fields, in gymnasiums. Perhaps times are changing, but in the history of humanity, until recently, shouldering, being shouldered, and acquiring the skill to avoid shoulders has been a gendered activity. Girls have traditionally excluded someone from a group by talking; boys shove. Shouldering can be done playfully—as one can imagine the young men shouldering each other about as they arranged themselves for the photo. Perhaps there was a seventh young man who was shouldered out before the shutter clicked. For boys and young men, vulnerability to shoulders is among the ordinary difficulties of reality. A practical difficulty, it comes with being embodied. But then, shoulders are also where soldiers learn to shoulder the stock of a rifle. This is how they learn to shoulder other soldiers out of life— shouldered out of any further need for a shoulder. Still, even this extreme instance of being shouldered out is containable in thought, however regrettable the train of thought becomes. Humans shove each other about; we are aggressive animals. Nations go to war; sometimes we kill each other on a massive scale. Individual lives get caught up in historical catastrophe. We know "others die." We know "we shall eventually die." We know it can be "tragic." And yet the poet's invitation to gaze on a photo threatens to upend all that. The permanent contradictory horrors (that smile from the photo) shoulder out *one's own body from its instant and heat.* The poet reports his own body shouldered out: shoved from its place in time, released from the demand to keep its temperature at a differential from the environment. And yet the poet is still there to express it. Is he there to experience being shouldered out of a living body?

The philosopher's interest is about expressing an experience of the inadequacy of our concepts to encompass the reality they are meant to encompass. It derives from our being creatures who live with and through concepts. In our actions, we purport to understand what we are doing—and our understanding is conceptual in form. Similarly, we try to understand others and the world we inhabit—in conceptual terms. And yet there are experiences at the heart of human life that demand this form of understanding and, at the same time, threaten the fabric of intelligibility.

So, *death*. We cannot leave it alone. Ducks do not have the same concern for the bones of their ancestors as we have for the bones of ours.[8] All cultures have rituals and customs and narratives that take death into account. These practices and narratives have been part of our enduring efforts to live with death. The concept *death* arises in the context of these efforts. It is part of these efforts. We live with death by trying to comprehend it. Here, the point is not that we should somehow penetrate death's mysteries but simply that we have a concept—*death*—in terms of which we can find our way around what we do know, what we do not know, what we could not know, and so on.

Here enters room for a thought that if the concept *death* is part of our attempt to live with death, then perhaps it is part of our effort to *contain* death by making it intelligible. And that thought makes room for a suspicion that when it comes to facing death, *conceptuality itself* might serve as a tranquillizer. The point of the concept *death* is to be able to deploy it in judgments—judgments about death. These judgments are then brought into thoughtful relations with others. The experience of difficulty upends all this. So, take the most banal of such judgments—say, "All humans are mortal." Perhaps one is working through a textbook syllogism that concludes that Socrates is mortal. And then one looks at a photograph of six young men. The most ordinary of acts—yet, it seems to carry within it the power to explode the pretense of the concept *death* to be able to do what it is supposed to do. Judgment is rendered inadequate by a gaze at a photo.

Cora Diamond's essay is "The Difficulty of Reality *and the Difficulty of Philosophy*," and these are not two independent difficulties. Philosophy inherits a difficulty from the difficulty of reality, in Diamond's special sense. If philosophy's task is to find its way to be adequate to reality, how is philosophy to find its way to be *adequate to a fundamental inadequacy* in mind's effort to encompass reality? Diamond has shown that there is a tendency internal to philosophy, taken as a discipline, to evade this problem by sticking to its normal form of looking for arguments as though this were one more problem among others.[9]

Diamond's challenge, as I understand it, is to practical philosophy, and it may be expressed thus: Are there ways of living well with the recognition of the difficulty of reality, irrespective of whether that difficulty is actually experienced? For our situation is not that we have, as it were, a normal universe of happiness and unhappiness, with Priam's suffering at the outer bounds, and now we have discovered an even more distant planet of grief. The possibility of an experience of the difficulty of reality is there in our every step: it is ready to explode in an old family photograph, in a hamburger on our plate, in a poem we pick up, in a passing thought about justice.

Consider mourning. Mourning is typically what we do when faced with the death of a loved one. We tend to withdraw from ordinary routines, become absorbed in memories, and find ways to express our sorrow. Freud, as we have seen, took what we normally do and turned it into a signifier of health. Mourning becomes an appropriate response to death. But now consider Ted Hughes's poem: Is it an act of mourning, or is it a revolt against mourning, a disruptive declamation of the inadequacy of any such attempt to normalize such loss?

It was Freud who came up with the idea of a revolt against mourning. Perhaps the poet Ted Hughes can help us take another, different look at the Young Poet with whom Freud vehemently disagreed in his essay "On Transience" (see Chapter 2). In that fictitious "summer walk through a smiling countryside," a Young Poet and a friend take no joy in the surrounding natural beauty because it is all fated to extinction. Freud famously diagnoses a revolt *in the Poet's mind.* In response to present beauty, the Poet's imagination leaps ahead to a future time when that beauty is no more, and then that thought is used to shut down any enjoyment he might otherwise have experienced in the present. On Freud's reading, the Poet is attacking his own capacity to take joy in the present.[10]

But what if Freud's Poet were experiencing the difficulty of reality? The emphasis then should be not on what is going on in his mind but rather on the revolt against mourning itself. The Young Poet looking on those lilies is similar to Hughes, the poet, beholding the photograph. It is not so much about the future extinction of those lilies; rather, it is that the lilies serve as occasion for being *shouldered out.* The lilies manifest extinction—the extinction of everything—right there in them, in their present existence, and that is not an occasion for joy. The Young Poet is shouldered out of the assumption that the concept of *death* is adequate to comprehend the phenomenon. Mourning may provide routines to cope with terrible pain and loss. It may provide rituals, human company, and words of solace that have been tested through the ages. It may facilitate the slow transition from withdrawal and grief to re-engaging in life and the social world. But from the Young Poet's point of view, the entire institution of mourning is organized for the sake of normalization and evasion. It may facilitate return to life but on a false basis. This is the revolt, not the mere psychological reaction to fear of pain in the future. If this were the Young Poet's position, it would make sense that he be resolute in his disagreement with Freud.

Freud's encounter with the Poet would thus be a nonmeeting of the minds. Freud has no room for the thought that all the mourning rituals that occur across cultures and throughout human history should be regarded as essentially misleading and that, far from expressing human health, they should be warded off by resolute measures such as refusing to take pleasure even in a blooming lily.[11] From the Poet's perspective, mourning is deployed in a cover-up, an illusion of what it is appropriate for humans to do. Death, for the Poet, is a difficulty of reality: it is that before which the mind—through suffering, disorientation, fear and trembling, wounding, anxiety, and, perhaps, through laughter—experiences a fundamental inability to comprehend.

Ted Hughes's poem and Freud's essay have a similar structure. Both begin with the narrator picturing an idyllic scene. With Hughes, the narrator is looking at a photograph; Freud's words give a snapshot of a summer stroll. Then, there is the outbreak of war catastrophe. And then the narrator is looking back, trying to say what it all means. At this point, poem and essay wildly diverge. Freud's essay strives for an interpretive unity that the poem threatens to bust apart.

"I believe," Freud says, "those who . . . seem ready to make a permanent renunciation because what was precious proved not to be lasting, are simply in a state of mourning for what is lost."[12] Since mourning, however painful, comes to a "spontaneous end," we ought to expect them eventually to recover from their outlook. Freud purports to take all possibilities into account. Those who disagree with him are either irrational, as is the Young Poet in the revolt *in his mind* (a psychological condition), or they are mourning and will eventually get over it. There is no room for the thought that war discloses more than a natural cycle of civilization–destruction–renewal: that it wounds some with the experience of the inadequacy of the human mind to make sense of reality. Freud takes the fact that he can hold onto his position even in times of war to be evidence in its favor. But from this contrarian point of view, Freud's steadfastness shows that even in times of war, one can continue to avoid the experience of difficulty of realty.

This is an example of how the difficulty of reality can pose a difficulty for psychoanalysis. How do we resist the temptation to assume that if the poet is in revolt against mourning, this must be understood exclusively in psychological terms?

It helps to entertain in imagination the thought that the very idea of mourning is outrageous. The idea of mourning seems to presuppose that justice requires us to return from our preoccupations with the dead. Justice, that is, in the ancient Greek sense of *dike:* a restoration of order. Freud called it health. Mourning has internal to it the idea of eventually restoring our proper balance in the relation of the living to the dead. In a sense, that is what looking at a photograph is all about: reaffirming that that was *before,* that was when they were still alive, that was when they did not know and could not know what we *now* do know and cannot but know, but who, like them, cannot fathom what is to befall us or our loved ones *later.* It is one of the countless ways we maintain our balance with respect to reality. And that is what we do, we who are alive and fated to orient ourselves in time and space, in history, in reality. The revolt against mourning is a revolt against the idea that anything remotely like justice *or injustice* could apply when it comes to living with dead loved ones. Even to think a terrible injustice has been done is to bring our thought into some kind of alignment with thoughts of rectification and restoration. Achilles is in his tent, sulking at the massive injustice done to him. He refuses to accept that any of the gifts brought to him could possibly provide adequate compensation. For Achilles, *as he is standardly received,* nothing could be enough. But now there opens a possibility for a different interpretation. *Our* Achilles experiences the utter inadequacy of the concepts *justice and injustice* to encompass reality. His is a revolt against mourning itself.

7

Gratitude and Meaning

Gratitude as a Puzzle

Toward the end of her career, Melanie Klein published "Envy and Gratitude," and by now, this essay is a classic in psychoanalytic literature.[1] It is written in a style of summing up a lifetime of psychoanalytic experience. The article spurred an outpouring of research on envy and, indeed, influenced important shifts in clinical technique, but very little has been written on gratitude.[2] We are thus living with an unworked-out inheritance.

Why, in particular, should *gratitude* be placed at one pole on the axis of human well-being and suffering? Why not joy or happiness or Stoic acceptance or simply satisfaction? The early bird catches its worm and, as far as we can tell, is satisfied and moves on. A person goes to a café and gets an espresso. It is delicious; the person is pleased. Someone enters the biggest contract of her life to buy a house. She is dependent on lawyers, real-estate agents, bankers, and a seller, none of whom she knows well. It all goes well; she feels relief and joy. In all these vignettes, there would have to be more to the story to explain why gratitude might be the appropriate response. But what is this more?

Health is the unconscious of psychoanalysis. There is a tendency, going back to Freud, to focus on pathology and leave the question of health as background. It also makes sense that clinicians should be more interested in envy. Psychoanalysts respond to people who come to them in pain. Their patients are often wounded and aggrieved, defended with self-destructive strategies, unconsciously determined to repeat (in the bad sense) failures again, unto eternity. Clinicians are on the receiving end of envious attacks, often painful, undermining, and confusing. They want to understand what is going on and figure out how to respond. Gratitude when it does occur is gratifying, and there is a tendency just to enjoy it and not examine it all that much.[3]

There is, I suspect, another reason for silence. Klein extends the concept *gratitude* so as to include infantile experience and unconscious mental activity. It is difficult to know what this could mean in any case, but especially difficult if one does not have the adult, conscious concept in view. "Analysis," Klein says, "makes its way from adulthood to infancy, and through intermediate stages back to adulthood, in a recurrent to-and-fro movement."[4] For Klein, there is directionality in psychoanalytic work. If one wants to keep track of direction, it is good to have a conception of the adult version in mind. One needs to know what the extension is an extension of.

In effect, Klein has laid down a challenge: how to understand gratitude as occupying a central place in human flourishing. The word "gratitude" is used in a variety of ways, and I am not going to provide a survey. Instead, I shall pick up a thread that goes back to Aristotle that fills out the picture and makes good sense of Klein's hypothesis. At the end of the paper, I shall turn to Wittgenstein.

Aristotle on Gratitude

Aristotle's account of gratitude has served as an influential historical paradigm, though it has often been misunderstood.

Aristotle thought gratitude was an emotion (*pathos*). Perhaps surprisingly, he treats the emotions in a social and political context. Emotions, he says, "are those things due to which people, by undergoing change, differ in their judgments, and that entail pain and pleasure—for example, anger, pity, fear, and other such things. . . ."[5] The *Rhetoric,* where the emotions are discussed, aims to teach public figures—orators and legislators—how to persuade an audience. A person who understands how emotions work will be able to shape the atmosphere in which decisions are made. As Aristotle says, "we do not deliver judgments in the same way when we are grieving and rejoicing, or loving or hating."[6] Here are three important features of emotions in Aristotle's account. First, human emotions are properly understood in the context of social life. They are a response to a prior event, and given our political and social nature, that prior event must usually be understood in social terms. So, for example, consider Aristotle's account of anger:

> Let anger be desire involving pain, for apparent revenge, because of apparent contempt on the part of someone un- fitted to treat the person himself, or of one of those close to him, with contempt. If then, this is what anger is, the angry person must always be angry at some particular individual . . . because the individual has done or is going to do something to him or one of those close to him, and all anger must

entail some sort of pleasure, namely, the one from the hope of being revenged.[7]

In short, you hurt me, and now I am angry at you and seek revenge (and I take pleasure in anticipating it). Or you are a bully and scare me, but now I have gone through years of training in martial arts and formed a menacing gang, and you no longer scare me. Indeed, I am confident. The emotion is an intermediate moment in a social dynamic. It takes itself to be a proper response to a prior event and also directs the agent toward some form of social action.

Second, emotions have cognitive and judgmental structure. Anger makes a claim for its own legitimacy: it takes itself to be justified. My heart may pound, my mind race with thoughts of revenge, but should I discover I made a mistake in thinking you harmed me, my anger ought to diminish. Third, although emotions have judgmental structure, in an important sense they are prior to judgment. An angry jury is likely to come to a harsher judgment than one that is more kindly disposed. The emotion shapes a field of orientation prior to rational calculation and judgment.

Gratitude, in Aristotle's account, is an emotion, but it has a special place in the social network. Gratitude is a response to a favor (*kharis*), but Aristotle here defines "favor" in a particular way: "Let a *favor* then in the sense in which the person who has received it is said to be grateful, be a service provided to one in need, not in return for anything, nor in order that the provider get something, but in order that the recipient get something."[8] So, gratitude, like the other emotions, takes its place in a social context. The benefactor recognizes a need in another person. These can be desires that arise in the agent (say, hunger) or some problem that person is facing in the social world.[9] The benefactor enters in response to the agent's need—and satisfies it. Gratitude is the emotional response to that benefaction, but that is not all. Gratitude is a response *to a favor*—and in this context, a favor is not only the satisfaction of the need, but also one that is "not in return for anything, or in order that the provider get something, but in order that the recipient get something." So, it is characteristic of gratitude that it acknowledges that no strings are attached. As David Konstan, in his book *The Emotions of the Ancient Greeks,* explains: "The emotion of gratitude is distinct from the act of reciprocation: it is felt, not due as compensation. . . . The sentiment of course *sustains* the social system of reciprocity, but has its own grammar and role. *Gratitude is never owed.* Gratitude was a response to the receipt of a benefit that had been bestowed precisely with no ulterior intention of gain on the benefactor's part. . . ."[10] So, part of what it is to "feel" gratitude is to appreciate not just the gift but also the generosity that motivated it and is manifest in it. In effect, the beneficiary receives a double gift from the benefactor: the satisfaction of the original need and, in addition, the gift of freedom from the normal social economy of gift and (expected) reciprocation.[11] On this conception of gratitude, then, there is no such thing as a debt of gratitude. And gratitude is more than a response to a gift: it is an emotional *recognition* that there is no pressure whatsoever for reciprocation. That is part of what the person is grateful for.

So, there is a fascinating twist in Aristotle's account of gratitude as an emotion. In the classic treatment, emotion is an intermediate stage between prior event and social response:

Prior Event	Emotion	(Social) Response	Hoped Outcome
Insult / Injury	Anger	Revenge / Punishment	Justice (restored)
Scary threat	Fear	Flight / Avoidance	Safety (restored)

But with gratitude we seem to have:

Prior Event 1	Prior Event 2	Emotion	(Social) Response	Hoped Outcome
Need	Response: Favor	Gratitude	?	?

I shall discuss the question marks presently, but for now, notice how different this structure also is from the normal economy of gift and reciprocation:

Prior Event	Emotion	(Social) Response	Hoped Outcome
Invitation to dinner "Gift"	Many possible: normal thanks, resignation, irritation, boredom, excitement, etc.	Bring wine Invite back	Harmonious social life

In this economy, it does not deeply matter what the intermediate emotion is, as long as it does not interfere with the cycle of exchange. With gratitude, by contrast, the emotion is crucial, and there is something open-ended about what comes next. Gratitude may facilitate the development of love, friendship, family, or community relations but with this twist: it works via recognition that nothing is required or expected in return.

Of course, the word "gratitude" can be used for a variety of emotional responses, linked by family resemblance. So, it is possible to call the normal economy of gift and reciprocation a structure of "gratitude." But there is this danger in doing so: one might be tempted in a reductionist and hermeneutically suspicious spirit to say that this is what "gratitude" is really all about. One thereby *covers over* the special sense of gratitude that Aristotle isolated and which I am trying to bring to light.

There is also all sorts of room for misfire. A person may not experience gratitude in response to a genuine benefaction. Indeed, she may defensively guard against it. Or she may be too prone to feel gratitude in response to seduction or manipulation. But that is just to say that there is something to *getting it right*. Gratitude, like the other emotions, implicitly makes a claim to its own legitimacy. When it is getting it right, gratitude manifests understanding of oneself and the world one inhabits. The world has been gracious, and one is free of any expected cycle of reciprocation. Ironically, it is precisely this recognition of freedom that motivates one to reciprocate, but in a special way, namely, with gratitude.

So, perhaps we can fill out the chart of gratitude thus:

Prior Event 1	Prior Event 2	Emotion	(Social) Response	Hoped Outcome
Need	Response: Favor	Gratitude	Expression of gratitude	?

It is internal to gratitude that it recognizes that nothing further is required. *Even gratitude* is not required or asked for, but that is part of why gratitude takes itself as an appropriate response. Gratitude honors the generosity of the benefactor by acknowledging it, and the form of acknowledgment is allowing itself (i.e., the expression of gratitude) to be sufficient response. By way of contrast, an angry person may let others know, by his anger, that he is angry. But the aim of anger is not simply to let others know how he feels; it is to seek punishment and restore justice. The person who feels gratitude, though, is motivated by his gratitude to let the benefactor know of his gratitude precisely as the appropriate form of response: one that accepts and acknowledges that no reciprocation is called for. Gratitude expresses gratitude for that too. In a way, gratitude protects the realm of generosity by recognizing it as such and not treating the benefaction as part of the normal economy of gift and (expected) reciprocation. It is a recognition (and acceptance) that nothing beyond itself is called for. This is important, for an immediate reciprocation of the normal sort does not sufficiently acknowledge the breadth and depth of the favor, namely, that it was given without interest in reciprocation, for the beneficiary's own sake. Of course, people who are beneficiaries of such favors and who experience gratitude may thereby want to give gifts in return. They may become motivated to be beneficiaries to others. But in the case we are considering, all this begins with gratitude and its recognition of freedom from the obligations of reciprocation.

There is this additional element that lends beauty on both sides of the benefactor–beneficiary relationship. The benefactor satisfies the original need—but in bestowing the favor wants nothing back in return. The beneficiary recognizes the gift *as a favor* and thereby understands that nothing further is required (thus the gratitude) but in the same act honors that favor by responding with gratitude.

Now consider a person who has developed a stable psychic capacity to experience gratitude on appropriate occasions—that is, in response to a genuine occurrence of a benefaction for this person's own sake. This is more than gratitude as an emotion; it is *gratitude as a characteristic way of being in the world* when the appropriate occasions arise. In an Aristotelian spirit, we can imagine this capacity emerging from repeated experiences of good nurturing in childhood, in particular habituation into benefactions and gratitude. This person would, first of all, have developed a capacity to understand what is happening in the world around her, at least with respect to this sort of gift. Internal to her emotional response would be grasping the truth. Gratitude, so understood, becomes a form of truthfulness: accurately understanding this portion of the world and responding appropriately.

Second, gratitude involves a recognition of one's freedom from obligation of reciprocation. Of course, there are some structures of reciprocation and obligation that are crucial to our flourishing, notably those involved in living a just life. For Aristotle, the *polis* is not just a social organization (as is a hive of bees or pack of wolves) but a society organized around a conception justice and flourishing. The *polis* is a social organization in which things are exchanged and tasks shared on the assumption (more or less realized) that citizens are participating in a just distribution of contributions and benefits. So, some structures of reciprocation are important and good. But, in addition, there is something special about there being a realm in which one can receive a gift and yet be freed from any obligation to reciprocate—and yet even further one can opt not to go any which way (e.g., take the gift for granted) but rather respond appropriately, namely, with gratitude.

Third, the experience of feeling and manifesting gratitude is itself gratifying. One feels pleasure in acknowledging and thanking another for their generosity.

If we consider these three conditions together, it becomes plausible to think of gratitude—not just the emotion but the stable psychic capacity to experience gratitude appropriately—as partially constitutive of human flourishing. Gratitude emerges as a capacity to recognize love and care in the world (when and where it occurs) and to respond in an appropriate fashion with a loving thanks that acknowledges the generosity as such. Given that the experience is itself pleasant, it also makes sense to think of gratitude as a condition of our happiness (in the sense of eudaimonia).

We can now offer a conjecture on how to fill out the chart of gratitude:

Prior Event 1	Prior Event 2	Emotion	(Social) Response	Hoped Outcome
Need	Favor	Gratitude	Expression of gratitude	? Intimacy? Play? Friendship? Love? Repetition? Mourning?

I shall discuss various aspects of the Hoped Outcome, but for now, note that there is a certain open-endedness and indefiniteness that marks it. Both the benefactor of a favor and the beneficiary who experiences and expresses gratitude recognize that they are in a realm of freedom—freed from the normal social routines of gift and reciprocation. By expressing gratitude, the beneficiary acknowledges that they are in this realm *together*. What should they then do? Part of their freedom is their recognition that that is up to them. There are no set rules to follow. Let me though mention repetition. The hope is not that the beneficiary shall forever keep receiving gifts from the benefactor. Rather, it is a hope that the open space of generosity and its recognition can be a cycle of life, the way things basically are—or, if lost, can be recovered. Restoration is possible. It need not be explicitly formulated or consciously experienced as such but is manifest in the living. While one hopes there will be developments, re-creations, and repairs, there is also a hint of timelessness that characterizes this cycle. May the realm of generosity and its acknowledgment repeat itself unto eternity.

Melanie Klein on Gratitude

Let us now consider Melanie Klein's paradigm of gratitude in infantile experience. This essentially involves the imaginative life of phantasy. While there will be complex interweavings with later adult experience, infantile experience is preverbal: "All this is felt by the infant in much more primitive ways than language can express. When these pre-verbal emotions and phantasies are revived in the transference situation, they appear as 'memories in feelings' . . . and are reconstructed and put into words with the help of the analyst. . . . In fact, we cannot translate the language of the unconscious into consciousness without lending it words from our conscious realm."[12] So, infantile gratitude cannot have all the articulation of an emotion in Aristotle's sense. But it should have a broadly similar structure as *that from which* the conscious adult emotion emerges.

Klein's method was multifaceted. She drew upon the play, anxiety, and creative activity of infants as well as verbal reports of those who had only recently emerged into language speaking. She also focused on the "memories in feelings" that emerged in clinical treatment of adults—which she took to be remnants of infantile experience transformed over time by phantasy. She drew on childhood memories, as well as problems her patients faced in the social world and their seemingly infantile ways of negotiating them. It was like solving a polynomial equation all at once. And then there is an imaginative retrospection on how all of this could be alive in some form in the prelinguistic emotional life of the infant. Thus, infantile emotions are not altogether out of reach—though they do require our imaginative engagement and tolerance for putting things into words that, strictly speaking, do not fit into them. The paradigm, then, should not be thought of as absolutely accurate account but as orienting us in the direction of early emotional life.

The paradigm scene for Klein is the infant at the breast:

> . . . the breast is instinctively felt to be the source of nourishment and therefore, in a deeper sense, of life itself. This mental and physical closeness to the gratifying breast in some measure restores, if things go well, the lost prenatal unity with the mother and *the feeling of security that goes with it* . . . *in this way the mother is turned into a loved object.* It may well be that his having formed part of the mother in the pre-natal state contributes to *the infant's innate feeling that there exists outside him something that will give him all he needs and desires. The good breast is taken in and becomes part of the ego, and the infant who was first inside the mother now has the mother inside himself.*[13]

Even the well-nurtured and well-natured infant goes through periods of anxiety and terrible fears, but when things are going well, the infant's experience in a good and loving feed is wondrous and wonderful. Since this is a preverbal experience, it makes sense that something enigmatic permeates this sense of goodness. Nevertheless, certain characterizing moments come through. I follow Klein in using language while acknowledging that we are trying to capture infantile states of mind.

First, there is an experience of *transcendence*—not supernatural but as pointing beyond itself. The breast, as Klein says, is experienced not just in terms of the immediate satisfaction of hunger but as a *source*, pointing in the direction of *a source of life itself*. This is an experience of something beyond the immediate—something full and rich and generous.

Second, there is a pervasive sense of *security*. This is tied to the experience of transcendence. As Klein says, the infant experiences something outside him that will give him "all he needs and desires." The emphasis here is on *all*: this is not just about a momentary satisfaction of need. The temporality of this experience is crucial. Although the experience of security is itself transient, *while one is in it*, one feels safe *through time*. One cannot feel safe if one is worried that the current wonderful state will explode in the next moment. There is a sense of release from the vagaries of time.

Third, there is an experience of *repetition*—that something primordially good has been restored. A lost unity has returned. These are early steps in building confidence that the good, if lost, can return.

Finally, there is *internalization* of and identification with the enigmatic good. In phantasy, the "good breast," or the mother, is taken in along with the mother's milk. There is now a good object inside—something the infant can identify with and take comfort from as a part of herself. The infant has elementary feelings of something fundamentally good *in her* as well as the world around her. It raises the infant's spirits, intrigues and prompts the first attempts at emulation, *swallowing and taking all that goodness in*.

Indefiniteness pervades the experience. Klein thinks that the infant is object directed from the beginning of life. But what does this mean? She also says that in the infant's mind, there is "already *some indefinite connection* between the breast and other aspects of the mother." And the breast, for the infant, is not "merely a physical object." Unconscious phantasies "imbue the breast with qualities going far beyond the actual nourishment it affords."[14]

Containing and Knowing

I want to turn to those who have developed Klein's thought. Wilfrid Bion has drawn our attention to how transformative the infant's experience of being at the mother's breast is.[15] The infant is getting hungry and thus *ever more full* of bad feelings: gnawing hunger pains, bodily feelings of anxiety (the somatic feels of heart pounding, panting breath), and the auditory and somatic feels of crying. Overwhelmed with anxiety, the infant splits off these bad feelings and projects them into the mother or what is experienced of her, what Klein calls "the good breast." The infant now becomes anxious that these bad feelings have poisoned the breast and have turned it bad—into something the infant needs to fear. This is what Klein calls *projective identification:* in phantasy, the bad feelings are now placed inside the mother, affecting her identity.[16] She may now be a bad, angry, vindictive mother. These phantasies, Bion stresses, have a communicative function. They can be efficacious. Let us consider a simplified example. The infant, full of bad feelings, screams them out. Infant screams are disturbing to adults, especially the parents. They are not experienced simply as loud noises. They stir up feelings—worry, frustration, anxiety, anger, exhaustion. In some sense, the infant is getting it right: the infant *has* put bad feelings into mother, and now she might be bad. But in the idealized scene, instead of screaming back or going crazy with rage, the loving mother "contains" these feelings of the infant and, in her "reverie," transforms them into comfort and thought.

"Everything is all right my darling one, *you are just hungry*, everything is going to be all right; *here. . . .*" With that, the infant is enveloped in the smells and feels of a loving, comfortable mother, and is given a good feed. The infant is *filled up* with good. "In this way," Ronald Britton says, "something which in the infant which was near-sensory and somatic was transformed into something more mental by the mother which could be used for thought or stored for memory."[17] In this exchange, the infant *gets back so much more and so much better* than the infant gave. The infant expelled the bad bits—the angry, hungry nuggets—and got back calming food informed by love, language, and understanding of what the infant is feeling. This tends to dispel the prior anxiety. Bion describes this transformation in an algebraic language: the beta elements of the bodily not yet represented are transformed into alpha elements of thought and emotion. This transformative process Bion calls alpha function. I am concerned that this vocabulary flattens the wondrousness of the transformation. The important point to recognize here is that *the container is never just a container, and the contained is never just contained*. The "container" is active in developing the emotions, thoughts, and phantasies, maturing them through love and care. In the mother's "return" of these transformed emotions to the infant, their relationship deepens.

If we consider the adult emotion of gratitude, it is permeated with intelligibility all parties can recognize. A beneficiary may be surprised that a donor has decided to give a gift, but the *need–favor–gratitude* connection is clear. In the infantile case, by contrast, there is room for surprise, wonder, and delight that *intelligibility itself* is coming into view. In addition to the feed (which the infant was seeking though not understanding that as such), the infant is lovingly *informed* of what this is all about. There is also the possibility of a retrospective transformation of the prior bad feeling. Over time, the infant comes to understand that the "bad feeling" hunger is not all that bad; it is part of a cycle of living that one can come to understand, accept, and, on occasion, enjoy.

In effect, in response to the original cry, the infant receives back a quadruple gift: first, the satisfaction of the hunger; second, a meaningful interpretation of what has been happening; third, meaningfulness itself, a sense that the world is such that it opens itself up to being understood; fourth, that this is all given out of love and for the infant's sake. This all counts as a *favor* in Aristotle's sense. In particular, meaningfulness itself is a gift provided "not in return for anything, nor in order that the provider get something, but in order that the recipient get something." There is a dawning recognition on the infant's part of getting so much more—a gift of loving intelligibility from an indefinite other that, for lack of better words, we call "the good breast" or "mother" or "the world."

This recognition is an emotional link, and Bion thought it was the origin of thinking. Edna O'Shaughnessy describes it thus:

> This first form of thinking strives to know psychic qualities, and is the outcome of early emotional events between a mother and her infant which are decisive for the establishment—or not—of the capacity to think in the infant. Bion's theory, which carries the interesting implication that knowledge of the psychological precedes knowledge of the physical world, represents a new understanding of thinking as one of the fundamental links between human beings, a link which is fundamental also for the forming and functioning of a normal mind. . . . Bion does not mean some abstract mental process. His concern is with thinking as a human link—the endeavour

to understand, comprehend the reality of, get insight into the nature of, etc., oneself or another. Thinking is an emotional experience of trying to know oneself or someone else.[18]

Gratitude, then, is among the infant's first efforts to get to know mother and self. It is in the mode of emotional thinking through the meaning of this experience, precisely in experiencing it as a loving gift of meaningfulness. It is also, in the same act, the deepening of an emotional, loving relationship. The baby had felt bad feelings, and screamed them out into the mother, but the mother understood them as an expression of need: not as something that is bad and makes the baby bad but as something that needs to and can be responded to. The mother conveyed that understanding back at the same time as she was satisfying the need, so that now, and ever more fully, the baby can understand self and world as basically good, even when feeling bad. The baby's gratitude is a reaction to the gift of understanding and invites the mother to give more. The philosopher Stephen Darwall calls gratitude an "opening of the heart."[19] He makes an important point about the reciprocity of "thank you" and "you're welcome" that I want to adapt to the early mother–infant relationship. In the experience of gratitude, the infant's "thank you" is at the same time saying "you're welcome"—welcome to explore my heart. This is what Klein calls the establishment and consolidation of the good internal object: a sense of oneself as having sufficient inner goodness. Here is an elementary link between gratitude and generosity. Gratitude itself *feels good*, it feels as though the *good is inside*, and it feels as though one can share it (via expressing that very feeling) without a sense of loss.

For Klein, healthy emotional development consists in recurring loss and restoration of the good object. There are inevitable frustrations and deprivations and failures of the world to meet our needs and desires. Within us, there are inevitable conflicts between love and hate, jealousy, desire and envy; there is also anxiety and fear of fragility. The good internal object—our confidence in our own goodness—is vulnerable, as is our confidence in the world as a sustaining environment.[20] But with a series of repetitions of restoration of the good object, a sense of confidence is built up, so that even in times of loss, there will be a return. This is repetition (in the good sense): confidence that restoration will be new.

It begins with an infantile leap of faith. It "sounds paradoxical," Klein says, "but since . . . integration is based on a strongly rooted good object that forms the core of the ego, a certain amount of splitting is essential for integration." Earliest experience consists in splitting into good and bad aspects, and primordially opting for the good:

> If the good object is deeply rooted . . . [this] allows the all-important process of ego integration and object synthesis to operate. Thus a mitigation of hatred by love can come about in some measure. . . . As a result, the identification with a good and whole object is the more securely established; and this also lends strength to the ego and enables it to preserve its identity as well as a feeling of possessing goodness of its own . . . full identification with a good object goes with a feeling of the self-possessing goodness of its own.[21]

Gratitude, then, even in its infantile form, is itself acknowledgment that one is on the receiving end of a loving gift, with nothing demanded in return. And that itself is an integrating experience: in acknowledging one has received the good, one welcomes the good.

Through repeated internalizations and identifications with the good object, one develops a sense of oneself as having the inner resources not only to experience and express gratitude but also to be a gratifying source for others. This cycle of repetition builds confidence—a sense that even when the good is under threat, even lost, the good will return. In this way, gratitude facilitates psychic integration—a capacity to hold these different moments of life together.

Meaningfulness Is Itself a Gift

On the paradigm we have been examining, the development of the capacity to understand—oneself, others, and the world—is itself a gift. It comes *as extra* and *with love* and thus *without further demand for reciprocation*. Of course, that is precisely what opens up a realm of reciprocity—an opening of hearts toward each other. Gratitude is the form of thanks that acknowledges this freedom from demand and gives thanks for that.

In this context, let me say a word about psychoanalysis. The psychoanalyst Ronald Britton said of one of his patients that what she wanted from him was *sanctuary* and *meaning*.[22] This seems to me a deep truth about the psychoanalytic situation generally. Psychoanalysts are responders to problems of heart and mind. Their task is repetition of earlier paradigms that, for whatever reasons, did not work out well. In effect, this is a transformation: from the "bad" repetitions of the past to the "good" repetition of re-creation and renewal and meaningfulness. Analysands get back *themselves*—their own thoughts and feelings, transformed by the "containing" functions of the analyst working with them in an analytic relationship. With practice, good fortune, steadfastness, and so on, analysands will internalize and take over the analyzing function for themselves. They can begin to create their own meanings, in the company of others, with a thoughtful and creative spirit.

But with gratitude in view, I would like to make two additions to Britton's comment. Not only did his patient want *sanctuary* and *meaning*, she wanted sanctuary and meaning *from him* and *as a gift*, with absolutely no strings attached. She wanted *that very person*, her analyst, to be the source of meaning and safety and she wanted him to be a fit object of gratitude. She wanted him to be doing his analytic work for her sake. Obviously, most analysts need to get paid. It is good for analysands to recognize the reality of the situation in which they are living and so on. But in commending gratitude, I think Klein is saying that the analysand's desire is more than an infantile wish that needs to be analyzed. Whatever the infantile origins, the analysand is getting something right about her needs. And as repetition, this whole analytic relationship should be more and other than a normal one of service and exchange. It should be the re-creation of a special kind of gift experience, perhaps one that has never occurred before. A crucial aspect of analytic work is that there are no strings attached. How that is achieved is an ongoing challenge for psychoanalysis.

Wittgenstein on Ethics

We have been examining gratitude first as an *emotion* then as an aspect of human flourishing: a capacity of the psyche to respond with gratitude on appropriate occasions as they arise in life. Thus understood, gratitude is an aspect of *virtue* or *excellence* in being human. I conclude with one last account of gratitude as a *basic attunement* to the world. I shall do so via an account Ludwig Wittgenstein gives of his attitude toward meaningfulness.

In 1929, Wittgenstein gave a talk to the Cambridge Heretics, a society of students and dons at the University of Cambridge, that has come to be known as "A Lecture on Ethics."[23] But as one reads Wittgenstein's lecture, it becomes clear that it is essentially unclear what it is about. He begins with the claim that Ethics is the inquiry into what is good, but he adds: ". . . I could have said Ethics is the enquiry into what is valuable, or, into what is really important, or I could have said Ethics is the enquiry into the meaning of life, or into what makes life worth living, or into the right way of living. I believe if you look at all these phrases you will get a rough idea as to what it is that Ethics is concerned with."[24] Wittgenstein likens his method to a technology that was current in the photography of his day: superimpose an assortment of images of faces from an ethnic or national group and thereby produce a characteristic face of that group. Now we have technology that makes it possible to imagine taking an image of everyone in world and consolidating them into a single image. If one asks *who in the world this is the face of,* the answer is *no one.* Wittgenstein is building to the thought that Ethics is not about anything in the world— though in some uncanny sense "it" is ever present.

He says that each of the phrases he uses in his list—*good, valuable, meaningful life,* and so on—can be used in two senses: a "trivial or relative" sense, on the one hand, or an "ethical or absolute" sense, on the other. In a relative sense, a *good* swimmer for example can be explicated by a series of criteria that put one in the realm of winning an Olympic medal. But Ethics as Wittgenstein wants to talk about it is aiming at *good* in an "absolute sense." Good, period. No statement of facts, however comprehensive, can get to it. "There will simply be facts, facts, facts but no Ethics." Readers who have a feel for the infantile cropping up in adult life will sense it in how Wittgenstein continues: "I can only describe my feeling by the metaphor, that, if a man could write a book on Ethics which really was a book on Ethics, this book would, with an explosion, destroy all the other books in the world."[25] Wittgenstein is exquisitely aware that he cannot say what he wants to say. And he, better than anyone, has brought to light that this is not because of a psychological limitation on his part. He experiences himself as coming up against what language can do. But that does not stop him. His strategy for communicating is to put forward exemplary moments. What are the moments in his life when he finds himself tempted to talk about absolute or ethical value?

> . . . in my case, it always happens that the idea of one partic-
> ular experience presents itself to me which therefore is, in a
> sense, my experience *par excellence* and this is the reason why,
> in talking to you now, I will use this experience as my first
> and foremost example. (As I have said before, this is an en-
> tirely personal matter and others would find other examples
> more striking.) I will describe this experience in order, if pos-
> sible, to make you recall the same or similar experiences, so
> that we may have a common ground for our investigation. I
> believe the best way of describing it is to say that when I have
> it *I wonder at the existence of the world*. And I am then in-
> clined to use such phrases as "*how extraordinary that anything
> should exist*" or "*how extraordinary that the world should exist*."
> I will mention another experience straight away which I also
> know and which others of you might be acquainted with: it
> is, what one might call, the *experience of feeling absolutely safe*.
> I mean the state of mind in which one is inclined to say "*I
> am safe, nothing can injure me whatever happens*."[26]

Remember the psychoanalytic patient who sought *sanctuary* and *meaning*? Wittgenstein is the philosopher who experiences the wonder at the very being of meaning and sanctuary. He tries to explain: his wonder is not that the sky is blue, nor is it that the sky is not blue. If he were simply wondering about the sky being blue, he could launch a scientific inquiry into why it should appear such. Ditto if the sky were some other hue. But Wittgenstein's wonder is that *the sky is blue or not blue.* His wonder is at a tautology: that there should be meaningfulness *at all.* How could it be that there "is" meaningfulness? As Ethical, this is not the sort of question that can be addressed by scientific investigation, say, on the evolutionary selection of neural systems, or the development of the capacity for symbolization or into the "foundations of logic." Wittgenstein is quick to acknowledge that in trying to express himself, he is "misusing language," speaking "nonsense." This may seem too harsh about language's possibilities. But his point is this: a basic function of language is to render judgments about things in the world. To ask how there could be meaningfulness tends us in the direction of treating "meaningfulness" as one more object in the world into which we can now inquire, rather than its being a condition of worldliness itself. And "the world" is not an object in the world. Indeed, "it" is not in any sense an object. And yet our language, and thus our thought, pushes us in the direction of treating the being of beings as though it were another being.[27] Here, then, is another experience that resists being put in verbal form. And yet, Wittgenstein continues, this striving to say something reveals "a tendency in the human mind which I personally cannot help respecting deeply and I would not for my life ridicule."[28]

I suggest that Wittgenstein's Ethics is itself an expression of gratitude—not as an emotion directed to any particular benefaction *in the world* or toward any particular person ("inside" or "outside" the world) but as a fundamental attunement to being. In this basic attunement, meaningfulness itself is experienced as though it were an awesome gift—something so much more than the satisfaction of an "original need" and coming as it were with no strings attached. There is nothing we are obligated to do with it in return. Meaningfulness is that in which we live and understand ourselves, others, and the world at large. It is that in terms of which we relate to each other and, in particular, express gratitude as an emotion and as human capacity of the psyche, a virtue. Wittgenstein experiences the pull to express gratitude *for all of that.* It is gratitude for the very possibility of gratitude (and the being of everything else). This is his Ethics.

A Final Word on Ethics and Exemplars

In his novel *Diary of a Bad Year*, J. M. Coetzee has his author write: "The best proof we have that life is good, and therefore that there may perhaps be a God after all, who has our welfare at heart, is that to each of us, on the day we are born, comes the music of Johann Sebastian Bach. It comes as a gift, unearned, unmerited, for free."[29] So, the author responds to Bach's music with the experience of it being a gift and the thought that this is "the best proof we have" that life as a whole is good and a caring God the source. This response is itself an expression of gratitude. Of course, the "best proof" is no proof at all in the standard sense of proof. But what the author is saying, I think, is that there is an inference here that has some claim to legitimacy: from the gift of Bach's music, to the world (not just bits and pieces of it but the totality) being good—and thus to the thought that there may be a source of goodness to whom we might feel grateful.[30] In effect, the author claims that the move from gratitude *as an emotion* (directed toward Bach) to gratitude as *basic attunement* is justified.

Please feel free to continue this line of thought with examples from your own life, but allow me to continue with Socrates and Plato and Aristotle and Kierkegaard. I do feel gratitude *toward them*. I am astonished that they were so extraordinarily brilliant and so generous at the same time. (I am not here talking about how they treated their family, friends, or fiancée.) When I am working through an argument in an Aristotelian text, for example, and begin to understand it, my heart fills with delight, but not just because I am coming to understand. I feel myself retracing a route that was long-ago traveled by *this very person*—who in addition was willing to lay it out in a way that others could follow in the future in an open-ended way. A gift to people he could never meet.

But when I examine the gratitude I experience toward these figures, I realize it is not just about them. The gratitude is also for the very being of a world in which, whatever else goes on, we could all be in it and share in these magnificent achievements. Wittgenstein talked about absolute safety, the psychoanalytic patient about sanctuary; when I am in the company of these figures—a transient, yet recurrent state—loneliness is out of the question. This is part of an expanded idea of mourning that I have been working out throughout this book. It is an openness to being a beneficiary via activities of imagination and memory, receptiveness, and acknowledgment. And, to return to the beginning, this is a form of mourning attacked by those who say of the human endeavor in general, "*We will not be missed!*"

Wittgenstein says that this basic attunement, which I am calling gratitude, can underlie and express a religious attitude. And, as we have seen, Coetzee moves in a similar direction. I shall close with a brief comment about that. One can see here at least the possibility of integration of intense infantile experiences—preverbal—with profound adult experiences that themselves do not easily fit into words. Both are manifestations of human awareness of being in the world. Both express gratitude. And mercifully, we are by now past the Freudian illusion that if we can trace religious experience back to infantile sources, we can thereby explain it away.[31]

The experience of gratitude as basic attunement does not provide evidence of anything. But neither is its call silenced when one recognizes its deep roots in the human psyche. Those who experience it are bequeathed something enigmatic. It is internal to the grammar of gratitude that it is directed toward a benefactor. But what kind of sense can we make of this when our gratitude is no longer directed toward a benefaction in the world but rather toward "the world" in which magnificent benefactions occur? It is such experiences, I think, that occasion an impulse in the direction of prayer—at least, that form of prayer that is an expression of gratitude. For those who have never experienced gratitude as basic attunement, these reflections will seem misplaced. But those who have will recognize that there is an issue here that may be ignored but cannot in truth be talked away.

Notes
Acknowledgments
Index

Notes

1. We Will Not Be Missed!

1. If some would like to use the term "mourning" to describe certain forms of animal grief, I have no objection. I am not trying to regiment the language, but I shall be using "mourning" to isolate and describe the human forms of experiencing loss.

2. *The Simpsons,* Season 29 Episode 1, "The Surfsons," directed by Rob Oliver, written by Brian Kelley, aired October 1, 2017, on Fox.

3. Bernard Williams, "The Human Prejudice," in *Philosophy as a Humanistic Discipline,* ed. A. W. Moore (Princeton, NJ: Princeton University Press, 2006), 138.

4. Sigmund Freud, "Beyond the Pleasure Principle," in *The Standard Edition of the Complete Psychological Works of Sigmund Freud,* vol. 18 (London: Hogarth Press, 1984), 7–64.

5. Sigmund Freud, "Mourning and Melancholia," in *The Standard Edition of the Complete Psychological Works of Sigmund Freud,* vol. 14 (London: Hogarth Press, 1957), 243, emphasis added.

6. Freud, "Mourning and Melancholia," 243–244.

7. Sigmund Freud, "On Transience," in *The Standard Edition of the Complete Psychological Works of Sigmund Freud,* vol. 14 (London: Hogarth Press, 1957), 306–307, emphasis added.

8. See Hans Loewald, "Internalization, Separation, Mourning and the Superego," in *Papers on Psychoanalysis* (New Haven, CT: Yale University Press, 1980), 258.

9. D. W. Winnicott, "Transitional Objects and Transitional Phenomena," in *Playing and Reality* (New York: Routledge, 2002), 3.

10. Winnicott, "Transitional Objects," 17, Winnicott's emphasis.

11. Winnicott, "Transitional Objects," 18.

12. Bernard Williams, *Ethics and the Limits of Philosophy* (Cambridge, MA: Harvard University Press, 1985), 174–196.

13. Williams, *Ethics,* 177. See also Alasdair MacIntyre, *Ethics in the Conflicts of Modernity: An Essay on Desire, Practical Reasoning, and Narrative* (Cambridge: Cambridge University Press, 2016), 64–69, 84–85, 115–120, 136–138.

14. I am indebted to Gabriel Lear for helping me understand that these are not distinct meanings of a single word but aspects of a unified concept. See, for example, Gabriel Lear, "Aristotle on Moral Virtue and the Fine," in *The Blackwell Guide to Aristotle's Nicomachean Ethics,* ed. R. Kraut (Oxford: Wiley-Blackwell, 2006), 116–136; "Plato on Learning to Love Beauty," in *The Blackwell Guide to Plato's Republic,* ed. G. Santas (Oxford: Wiley-Blackwell, 2006), 104–124.

15. Aristotle, *Nicomachean Ethics* I.9, 1099b25–1100a1. *Aristotelis, Ethica Nicomachea,* ed. I. Bywater (Oxford: Clarendon Press, 1975). For an English translation, see *Aristotle: Nicomachean Ethics,* trans. C. D. C. Reeve (Indianapolis, IN: Hackett, 2014).

16. See Irad Kimhi, *Thinking and Being* (Cambridge, MA: Harvard University Press, 2018).

2. Transience and Hope

1. See D. W. Winnicott, *Playing and Reality* (London: Routledge, 2008), 1–34, 128–139.

2. Sigmund Freud, "On Transience," in *The Standard Edition of the Complete Psychological Works of Sigmund Freud,* vol. 14 (London: Hogarth Press, 1984), 305.

3. Freud, "On Transience," 307, emphasis added.

4. ". . . er brach auch unseren Stolz . . . unserer Respekt . . . unsere Hoffnungen . . .": Sigmund Freud, "Vergänglichkeit," *Gesammelte Werke,* vol. 10 (Frankfurt: S. Fischer Verlag, 1946), 360.

5. Freud, "On Transience," 305.

6. See Matthew von Unwerth, *Freud's Requiem: Mourning, Memory, and the Invisible History of a Summer Walk* (New York: Penguin, 2005); Herbert Lehmann, "A Conversation between Freud and Rilke," *Psychoanalytic Quarterly*

35 (1966): 423–427; Elvio Fachinelli, "Freud, Rilke and Transience," *European Journal of Psychoanalysis* 1 (2014), http://www.journal-psychoanalysis.eu/freud-rilke-and-transience/.

7. Lou Andreas-Salomé, *The Freud Journal*, trans. Stanley A. Leavy (New York: Basic Books, 1964), 169.

8. von Unwerth, *Freud's Requiem*, 4.

9. Freud, "On Transience," 305, emphasis added.

10. See Søren Kierkegaard, *Spiritual Writings*, trans. George Pattison (New York: HarperCollins, 2010), 85–112.

11. Freud, "On Transience," 306.

12. W. R. Bion, "Attacks on Linking," *International Journal of Psychoanalysis* 40 (1959): 308–315. See also Sebastian Gardner, *Irrationality and the Philosophy of Psychoanalysis* (Cambridge: Cambridge University Press, 2007); Jonathan Lear, "Restlessness, Phantasy and the Concept of Mind," in *Open Minded: Working Out the Logic of the Soul* (Cambridge, MA: Harvard University Press, 1998), 80–122.

13. Freud, "On Transience," 306–307, emphasis added.

14. "dem Laien": Freud, *Gesammelte Werke*, 359.

15. "*Dem Psychologen aber ist die Trauer ein grosses Rätzel . . .*": Freud, *Gesammelte Werke*, 360.

16. Freud, "On Transience," 307, emphasis added.

17. Hans Loewald, "Internalization, Separation, Mourning and the Superego," *Psychoanalytic Quarterly* 31 (1962): 483–504.

18. "Es steht zu hoffen": Freud, *Gesammelte Werke*, 361.

19. Jonathan Lear, *Radical Hope: Ethics in the Face of Cultural Devastation* (Cambridge, MA: Harvard University Press, 2006).

20. Sigmund Freud, "Remembering, Repeating and Working-Through," in *The Standard Edition of the Complete Psychological Works of Sigmund Freud*, vol. 12 (London: Hogarth Press, 1981), 145–156.

21. Søren Kierkegaard, *Repetition: An Essay in Experimental Psychology*, trans. Walter Lowrie (Princeton, NJ: Princeton University Press, 1941); *The Concept of Anxiety: A Simple Psychologically Orienting Deliberation on the Dogmatic Issue of Hereditary Sin*, trans. Alastair Hannay (New York: Norton, 2014).

3. Exemplars and the End of the World

1. Homer, *Iliad*, trans. Robert Fagles (New York: Viking Penguin, 1998), 605.

2. Aristotle, *Nicomachean Ethics* I.9, 1099b30–1101a1, emphasis added.

3. *koinônêsai: Nicomachean Ethics* I.9, 1100a1.

4. blessedness (*tó makárion*), nobility shining through (*dialámpei tó kalón*): *Nicomachean Ethics* I.10, 1100b29–31.

5. wretched (*áthlios*), base actions (*tá phaúla*): *Nicomachean Ethics* I.10, 1100b33–1101a8.

6. Linda Zagzebski, *Exemplarist Moral Theory* (New York: Oxford University Press, 2017), 10.

7. It is possible for an extraordinary person to happen upon the Christian Bible and be taken by it *straight back* to Jesus in all his exemplarity and be lit up and forever changed by the encounter. Even here, one might wonder about the local exemplars who helped open him up to this possibility: experiences with parents or siblings or beloved teachers. But let us leave that aside. We do not need an exception-less principle but a characteristic trait. *For the most part, local exemplars* open us up to experience the exemplarity of the greater cultural figures.

8. Søren Kierkegaard, *The Concept of Anxiety: A Simple Psychologically Oriented Deliberation in View of the Dogmatic Problem of Hereditary Sin* (New York: Norton, 2014), 53–55.

9. Zagzegski, *Exemplarist,* 2.

10. Zagzegski, *Exemplarist,* 66.

11. Søren Kierkegaard, *Repetition: An Essay in Experimental Psychology,* trans. W. Lowrie (Princeton, NJ: Princeton University Press, 1946), 34. In this text, the pseudonymous author Constantin Constantius is speaking.

12. Sigmund Freud, "Remembering, Repeating and Working-Through," in *The Standard Edition of the Complete Psychological Works of Sigmund Freud,* vol. 12 (London: Hogarth Press, 1981), 154.

4. When Meghan Married Harry

1. Richard Wheatstone, "Meghan Markle & Prince Harry Reveal They Secretly Married Three Days Before Wedding at Windsor Castle in Oprah Interview," *The Sun* (UK), March 8, 2021.

2. Lucy Campbell, "Archbishop of Canterbury: Harry and Meghan's Legal Wedding Was on Saturday," *The Guardian* (UK), March 30, 2021.

3. For what it is worth, I am most confident of this conditional: *if* they are married at all, the marriage occurred during the private exchange of vows, witnessed and supported by the Archbishop of Canterbury. I do not think they could have gotten married on the public occasion because they thought they were already married and took themselves to be going through a mere pretense

for the sake of the public, the royal family, and so on. My guess is that they are married.

4. For a practical example of this issue, see Jonathan Lear, "After 'After this . . .'," *Apsáalooke Women and Warriors*, ed. Nina Sanders and Dieter Roelstrate (Chicago: Neubauer Collegium, 2019).

5. Good Mourning in Gettysburg and Hollywood

1. Drew Faust, *This Republic of Suffering: Death and the American Civil War* (New York: Alfred A. Knopf, 2008), 69.

2. Gregory A. Coco, *A Strange and Blighted Land, Gettysburg: The Aftermath of a Battle* (Gettysburg, PA: Thomas Publications, 1995), 34.

3. Coco, *A Strange and Blighted Land*, 88.

4. Coco, *A Strange and Blighted Land*, 87.

5. Coco, *A Strange and Blighted Land*, 94.

6. Coco, *A Strange and Blighted Land*, 114–119; Faust, *This Republic of Suffering*, 99–100.

7. Coco, *A Strange and Blighted Land*, 108. But see Marc Charisse, "Bodies Still Buried on the Gettysburg Battlefield," *The Evening Sun*, July 5, 2013, https://www.pottsmerc.com/bodies-still-buried-on-gettysburg-battlefield/article_6c2e3e54-2298-58b5-a143-1e09f3e27c07.html.

8. Faust, *This Republic of Suffering*, 238.

9. See Gary Wills, *Lincoln at Gettysburg: The Words that Remade America* (New York: Simon and Schuster, 1992); Allen C. Guelzo, *Abraham Lincoln as a Man of Ideas* (Carbondale: Southern Illinois University Press, 2009); John Burt, *Lincoln's Tragic Pessimism* (Cambridge, MA: Harvard University Press, 2013).

10. Cora Diamond, "The Difficulty of Reality and the Difficulty of Philosophy," *Partial Answers: Journal of Literature and the History of Ideas* 1 (2003): 1–26. I discuss this essay in Chapter 6.

11. For an excellent example of a complete misunderstanding of my work, see Paul Kottman, "Playing with the Dead: A Response to Jonathan Lear," *Critical Inquiry* 46 (2019): 212–224. For my response, see Jonathan Lear, "Critical Response II: Difficulties with the Difficulty," *Critical Inquiry* 46 (2019): 225–235.

12. He wrote three copies afterwards. It is the last copy—the so-called Bliss copy, written in 1864—that has come to be memorialized as the definitive text. It is inscribed at the Lincoln Memorial.

13. Faust, *This Republic of Suffering*, 238.

14. Faust, *This Republic of Suffering*, 243.

15. Coco, *A Strange and Blighted Land,* 134–148.

16. Coco, *A Strange and Blighted Land,* 140–141. By Weaver's calculation, he was owed $11,000—which in contemporary dollars would be approximately $216,000.

17. There is a magnificent pyramid there made out of rough-hewn stones piled on top of one another—with the exception of a few rectangular blocks inserted into their midst with such inscriptions as "To the Confederate Dead" and "Memoria in Aeterna." The pyramid recalls Egypt and its cults of the living dead.

18. Both Faust and Coco quote from a letter Weaver wrote to Mrs. E. L. Campbell of Savannah Georgia on October 9, 1871: "If all could see what I have seen and know what I know I am sure that there would be no rest until every Southern father, brother and son would be removed from the North." Coco, *A Strange and Blighted Land,* 134, 391 fn. 111; Faust, *This Republic of Suffering,* 246.

19. See John Trowbridge, "The Wilderness," *The Atlantic Monthly* 17 (January 1866). And see Governor Ruben Fenton's entry in the *New York Times* discussion "The Burial of the Rebel Dead," January 30, 1868, p. 4. Both are discussed by Faust, *The Republic of Suffering,* 237–238. See also John Trowbridge, *The South: A Tour of Its Battlefields and Ruined Cities in 1865* (online: Big Byte Books, 2015).

20. Coco, *A Strange and Blighted Land,* 390, n. 89.

21. See Raymond Gaita, *A Common Humanity: Thinking About Love and Truth and Justice* (London: Routledge, 2013); Cora Diamond, "The Importance of Being Human," in *Human Beings,* ed. D. Cockburn (Cambridge: Cambridge University Press, 1991), 35–62; Bernard Williams, "The Human Prejudice," in *Philosophy as a Humanistic Discipline* (Princeton, NJ: Princeton University Press, 2006), 135–152.

6. The Difficulty of Reality and a Revolt against Mourning

1. Aristotle, *Nicomachean Ethics* I.10, 1100b21–1101a12.

2. Aristotle, *Nicomachean Ethics* I.11.

3. Cora Diamond, "The Difficulty of Reality and the Difficulty of Philosophy," *Partial Answers: Journal of Literature and the History of Ideas* 1 (2003): 1–26.

4. Diamond, "Difficulty of Reality," 2–3.

5. Diamond, "Difficulty of Reality," 2–3.

6. Martin Heidegger famously said of us that we are the beings in whose being our being is an *issue* for us. *Being and Time,* trans. J. Macquarrie and E.

Robinson (New York: Harper and Row, 1962), 32. *Sein und Zeit* (Tübingen: Max Niermeyer Verlag, 2001), 12.

7. Diamond, "Difficulty of Reality," 2.

8. Jonathan Lear, *A Case for Irony* (Cambridge, MA: Harvard University Press, 2014).

9. Diamond, "Difficulty of Reality," 4–9, 11–13.

10. Sigmund Freud, "On Transience," in *The Standard Edition of the Complete Psychological Works of Sigmund Freud*, vol. 14 (London: Hogarth Press, 1957), 304–307. See W. R. Bion, "Attacks on Linking," *International Journal of Psychoanalysis* 40 (1959): 308–315.

11. See Michael Thompson, *Life and Action: Elementary Structures of Practice and Practical Thought* (Cambridge, MA: Harvard University Press, 2008).

12. Freud, "On Transience," 307.

7. Gratitude and Meaning

1. Melanie Klein, "Envy and Gratitude," in *Envy and Gratitude and Other Works 1946–1963* (London: Hogarth Press, 1984), 176–235.

2. Edna O'Shaughnessy's paper "On Gratitude" is the beautiful exception. See *Envy and Gratitude Revisited*, ed. P. Roth and A. Lemma (London: Karnac, 2008), 179–191. Of the fourteen essays in the book, only O'Shaughnessy's is on the subject of gratitude. For examples of transformation of technique, see Betty Joseph, "Transference: The Total Situation," *International Journal of Psychoanalysis* 66 (1985): 447–454; "On Understanding and Not Understanding: Some Technical Issues," *International Journal of Psychoanalysis* 64 (1983): 291–298; "Projective Identification: Some Clinical Aspects," in *Psychic Equilibrium and Psychic Change: Selected Papers of Betty Joseph*, ed. M. Feldman and E. B. Spillius (London: Routledge, 1989), 168–180; Michael Feldman, "Projective Identification: The Analyst's Involvement," *International Journal of Psychoanalysis* 78 (1997): 227–241; "The Oedipus Complex: Manifestations in the Inner World and the Therapeutic Situation," in *The Oedipus Complex Today Clinical Implications*, ed. R. Britton and E. O'Shaughnessy (London: Routledge, 1989), 103–128; Richard Rusbridger, "Elements of the Oedipus Complex: A Kleinian Account," *International Journal Psychoanalysis* 85 (2004): 731–747; John Steiner, "The Interplay Between Pathological Organizations and the Paranoid-Schizoid and Depressive Positions," *International Journal of Psychoanalysis* 68 (1987): 69–80.

3. See Paul Gray, "On the Receiving End: Facilitating the Analysis of Conflicted Drive Derivatives of Aggression," *Journal of the American Psychoanalytic*

Association 48 (2000): 219–236; "'Developmental Lag' in for the Evolution of Technique for Psychoanalysis of Neurotic Conflict," *Journal of the American Psychoanalytic Association* 30 (1982): 621–655. See also Lawrence Levenson, "Superego Defense Analysis in the Termination Phase," *Journal of the American Psychoanalytic Association* 46 (1998): 847–866.

4. Klein, "Envy and Gratitude," 178.

5. Aristotle, *Rhetoric* II.1, 1378a19–21. Aristotle, *Rhetoric,* trans. C. D. C. Reeve (Indianapolis, IN: Hackett 2018). (Reeve translates *pathê* as "feelings" rather than as emotions.) For other translations, see *Art of Rhetoric,* trans. G. Striker (Cambridge, MA: Harvard University Press, 2020), and *The Complete Works of Aristotle,* vol. 2, ed. J. Barnes (Princeton, NJ: Princeton University Press, 1984), 2194–2207.

6. Aristotle, *Rhetoric* I.2, 1356a15–16.

7. Aristotle, *Rhetoric* II.2, 1378b28. 1378b1 (trans. Reeve), 56.

8. Aristotle, *Rhetoric* II.7, 1385a17–19 (trans. Reeve), 72. In other contexts, *kharis* is used more generally to mean favor in a broad sense, but in the discussion of gratitude, Aristotle is giving it a specialized meaning. For an excellent account, see David Konstan, *The Emotions of the Ancient Greeks: Studies in Aristotle and Classical Literature* (Toronto: University of Toronto Press, 2006), 156–168.

9. See Konstan, *Emotions,* 160, and Aristotle, *Rhetoric* II.7.

10. Konstan, *Emotions,* 167–168, emphasis added.

11. Marcel Mauss, *The Gift: The Form and Reason for Exchange in Ancient Societies* (New York: W. W. Norton, 2000).

12. Klein, "Envy and Gratitude," 179, n. 1.

13. Klein, "Envy and Gratitude," 178–179, emphasis added.

14. Klein, "Envy and Gratitude," 180.

15. Wilfrid R. Bion, *Learning from Experience* (London: Routledge, 1984); Ronald Britton, "Keeping Things in Mind," *New Library of Psychoanalysis* 14 (1992): 102–113; Edna O'Shaughnessy, "A Commemorative Essay on W. R. Bion's Theory of Thinking," *Journal of Child Psychotherapy* 7 (1981): 181–182.

16. These are the dynamics of the paranoid-schizoid position. For an introduction, see Hanna Segal, *Introduction to the Work of Melanie Klein* (Hove, UK: Routledge, 1988); Penelope Garvey and Kay Long, "Melanie Klein: Her Main Ideas and Some Theoretical and Clinical Developments," in *The Klein Tradition,* ed. P. Garvey and K. Long (Hove, UK: Routledge, 2018), 3–38; Melanie Klein, "Notes on Some Schizoid Mechanisms," *International Journal of Psychoanalysis* 27 (1946): 99–110.

17. Britton, "Keeping Things in Mind," 105.

18. O'Shaughnessy, "Bion's Theory of Thinking," 181.

19. Stephen Darwall, "Gratitude as a Second-Personal Reactive Attitude (of the Heart)," in *The Moral Psychology of Gratitude,* ed. R. Roberts and D. Telech (London: Roman and Littlefield, 2019), 139–159.

20. O'Shaughnessy, "On Gratitude," 89–91.

21. Klein, "Envy and Gratitude," 192.

22. Britton, "Keeping Things in Mind," 103.

23. Ludwig Wittgenstein, "A Lecture on Ethics," *The Philosophical Review* 74 (1965): 3–12.

24. Wittgenstein, "Ethics," 5.

25. Wittgenstein, "Ethics," 7.

26. Wittgenstein, "Ethics," 8 (emphasis added).

27. This is, of course, a central issue that runs through the work of Martin Heidegger. See, for example, *Being and Time,* trans. J. Macquarrie and E. Robinson (New York: Harper and Row, 2008) and *Pathmarks,* ed. W. McNeil (Cambridge: Cambridge University Press, 1998).

28. Wittgenstein, "Ethics," 12.

29. J. M. Coetzee, *Diary of a Bad Year* (London: Harvill Secker, 2007), 221.

30. See A. W. Mueller, "Virtuous Feelings? Three Grades of Emotional Rationality," *Philosophical Inquiries* 7 (2019): 71–100.

31. Jonathan Lear, "Morality and Religion," in *Freud* (London: Routledge, 2015), 190–208.

Acknowledgments

I am grateful to Jon Baskin, Laura Baudot, Matthew Boyle, David Bromwich, John Coetzee, Cora Diamond, Hanna Gray, Francis Grier, Irad Kimhi, Susan James, Ben Jeffery, Gabriel Lear, Sophia Lear, Jane Levin, Amy Levine, Kay Long, Emma Lunbeck, Alasdair MacIntyre, Ian Malcolm, Alfred Margulies, Anselm Mueller, Edna O'Shaughnessy, Robert Pippin, Quentin Skinner, Jonny Thakkar, Candace Vogler, and David Wellbery, who read some or all of the manuscript and offered valuable comments. I would also like to thank Anton Ford for teaching a course with me, "The End of Life," at the University of Chicago. An early version of the first chapter was presented as the David A. Carlson Lecture at the Western New England Institute for Psychoanalysis. It was a special pleasure to be able to say thank you in such a way to David, one of my important psychoanalytic teachers. I am honored to have been invited to give the David L. Wagner Distinguished

Lectures in the Humanities at the Newberry Library in Chicago. Abridged versions of the first three chapters were delivered in that series. David Wagner was a true humanist, and the Newberry Library is a great library open to the public. Earlier versions of some chapters have appeared in print. Chapter One was originally published online on March 16, 2021, in *The Point* as was Chapter Four, which was posted there on July 13, 2021. Both texts are reprinted here with minor edits. Much of Chapter Two was first published under the same title in *The International Journal of Psychoanalysis* (2021), 102:1, 3–15. Portions of Chapter Five were first published as "Gettysburg Mourning", *Critical Inquiry* (2018) 45: 97–121. Most of the text of Chapter Six is drawn from an article of the same title published in *European Journal of Philosophy* (2018) 26: 4, 1197–1208.

Index

Index

conversation, ix–x, 13–14, 24, 28–31, 68, 70, 72

coronavirus pandemic, 21–23, 25, 27, 40, 41, 42, 44

courage, 7, 18, 58

creativity, 7, 8, 18, 26, 28, 51, 55–56, 75, 129, 137–138

culture, ix, 2, 10, 14, 45–47, 49, 59, 60, 74–76, 80, 116; cultural achievement, 26, 35; and normativity, 20–21, 23, 71–72; and ritual, 3, 33, 91–92, 113

Darwall, Stephen, 135

death, 4, 6, 8, 12, 14–15, 20–22, 33, 62, 74, 82–89, 91–102, 106–117; death of God, 38

democracy, 2–3, 41, 87, 90–91

despair, 7, 9–10, 67

Diamond, Cora, 19, 72, 89; difficulty of reality, 89, 106–114, 116–118; loss of concepts, 72

dike, 117

ego ideal, 31, 34, 36–37, 51

emotion, 57, 67, 74, 108, 110, 121–129, 130, 133–135, 138, 142–143

end, 60, 87, 90–91; of democracy, 2–3; of life, ix, 2, 42; of political life, 87; of the world, 1–3, 6–7, 27, 41–42, 62

enigma, 16, 48–50, 92, 130–131, 144

envy, 119–120, 136

equality and inequality, 87, 90, 93, 99, 100–104

eudaimonia, 42, 70, 73, 77, 128

evil, 24, 39, 50, 73, 91–92

excellence, 41, 43–45, 52–53, 73, 77, 105, 138

exemplar, 42–45, 46–61, 63, 68, 76–77, 140, 142

failure, 31, 39, 47, 57, 59, 73, 90–92, 100, 102, 111, 120, 136

faith, 40, 136

fantasy, 5, 7–8, 15, 21–22, 30–31, 33, 40, 62–63

Faust, Drew, 82, 85, 94

fiction, 19, 29, 52–53, 73

flourishing, x, 12, 16–17, 39, 42, 46, 63, 73–75, 78–80, 120, 127, 138

fragility, 6, 25, 31, 37–38, 40, 136

freedom, 9, 58, 72, 75, 87, 90, 99, 100–104, 123, 125–128, 137. *See also* liberty

Freud, Sigmund, 5, 120, 144; *Civilization and Its Discontents,* 14–15; "Mourning and Melancholia," 10–12, 62–64, 117; "On Transience," 23–40, 115–117; "Remembering, Repeating, and Working-Through," 39, 56–57

future, 2, 5–7, 10, 22–23, 26, 32, 41, 61, 103, 115–116, 143

generosity, 55, 59, 97, 131; and gratitude, 123, 125–129, 135, 143; of interpretation, 48, 50, 53–54; as *kalon,* 16–18; and the value of humanity, 8, 73

Gettysburg, Battle of, 82–83, 91, 96, 100, 102

Gettysburg Address, 81–82, 86–90, 92–94, 97–99, 103–104

Gettysburg National Cemetery, 84–86, 95, 98, 101

gift, 118, 123–124, 126–128, 133–138, 142–143

gratitude, x, 51, 97, 119–129, 133–138, 141–144

grief, 3, 11–12, 17, 25, 33, 74, 110, 114–116, 121

habituation, 59, 126–127

happiness, 14–16, 39, 42–45, 70, 73, 105–109, 114, 119, 128; unhappiness, 39, 109, 114

Harry, Duke of Sussex, 66–71

health, ix, 10–12, 40, 41–42, 57–58, 62, 64, 115–117, 120, 135–136

Heidegger, Martin, 4

Hollywood Cemetery, 94–96, 100

Homer, *Iliad,* 42; Achilles, 42, 45, 118; Hector, 42; Helen, 45; Paris, 45; Priam, 42–45, 60–61, 108, 110, 114

hope, 7, 24–25, 38–40, 41, 80, 103–104, 128–129

Index

Hughes, Ted, 107–109, 111–112, 115–116
humanities, 35, 65, 68, 72–74, 75–79
humanity, 6, 38, 67–68, 73, 80, 97, 112
humor, 1–10, 18–19

idealization, 19, 92, 132
ideals, 33–36, 38, 39–40, 42, 51, 60, 67,
    74, 87, 90, 95, 99, 103–104
identification, 25–27, 32, 34, 36, 38, 43,
    62–63, 131–132, 136–138
imagination, 9, 17, 21, 23, 29–30, 34, 38,
    45, 49–50, 53–54, 66–68, 73–74, 80,
    103, 129–130, 143; and health, ix–x, 41,
    59–64; and mourning, 3, 12–13, 15,
    17, 22, 63, 77–78, 102, 115–117; and
    play, 4–5, 7, 15, 77–78; and repetition,
    39–40
imitation, 43, 47, 50, 68, 73, 131
inquiry, 49, 65, 68–69, 139, 141
intelligibility, 68, 106, 111, 113, 133–134
interpretation, 38, 48, 50–54, 75, 89, 118,
    134

Jesus, 46, 47
Jung, Carl, 28
justice and injustice, 2, 5, 6, 9, 39, 51, 55,
    72, 79, 82, 91, 114, 117–118, 125, 127

kalon, 15–19, 42–47, 48, 53, 54–55, 59–61,
    70–74, 76–80, 90–92, 97–100, 102
Kennedy, John F., 82
Kennedy, Robert, 82
Kierkegaard, Søren, 4, 40, 46–48, 50, 56,
    78, 143
King, Martin Luther, 82
Klein, Melanie, 119–121, 129–132,
    135–138

liberty, 87, 90, 99, 100–104
Lincoln, Abraham, 84–90, 92–94, 97–99,
    102–103
logos, 34
love, 74, 76, 124, 127, 128, 133–137; of
    ideals, 35–38; and mourning, 11–12, 17,
    25, 28, 33, 62–63; and the value of
    humanity, 8

Markle, Meghan, Duchess of Sussex, 65–72,
    75–76, 79
marriage, 65–70, 71–72, 75
Meade, George, 100, 102
meaning, x, 22, 24, 30, 35, 65, 71, 74–76,
    98; of exemplars, 61, 68; and the *kalon*,
    16–17; of life, ix, 65–68, 90, 102, 141–142;
    and mourning, 12, 89; and psychoanalysis,
    134–135, 137, 138
melancholia, 10–11, 62–63, 103
memory, 4, 6, 10, 18, 35, 87, 89, 129, 133,
    143; of exemplars, 48, 54–55; and
    memorializing, 92–95, 97–101; and
    mourning, 11–13, 15, 18, 38, 114
misanthropy, 9–10
modernity, 71–72
mourning, x, 3–4, 11–19, 33–39, 62–63,
    73–75, 77–78, 84, 87, 108, 114, 128, 143;
    anticipatory, 6–7, 27, 61; refusal to, 8–10,
    92; revolt against, 31–33, 115–118; and
    valorization, 92, 95–96, 100–103

neurosis, 39, 56–57
Nietzsche, Friedrich, 9
nonretaliation, 48, 50–51, 53–55
novelty, 56–58

Oedipus, 34–35
omnipotence, 5, 33
O'Shaughnessy, Edna, 134

pathology, 11, 40, 57–58, 120
phantasy, 129, 132–133
philosophy, ix, 9, 23, 50, 59, 73, 114
Pickett, George, 96, 97
Plato, 2–3, 63, 72, 79, 143; *Euthyphro*, 72
play, 4, 12–15, 21, 48–49, 54–56, 58,
    60–61, 63, 75, 77–78, 128, 129
pleasure, 5, 6, 9, 32, 46, 55, 61, 67, 81, 98,
    116, 121–122, 127, 135
possibility, 30, 50–51, 52–53, 61, 63, 75,
    90, 91–92, 114, 118, 134, 142
pride, 16, 24–27, 32, 34, 36, 42, 107
projective identification, 132
psychoanalysis, ix–x, 6, 12–13, 29, 34, 38,
    40, 51, 56–57, 117, 119–120, 137–138

161

Index